Days of POWER

{ Part Two }

Copyright © 2006 Kabbalah Centre International

All rights reserved. No part of this publication may be reproduced or transmitted in any form or by any means, electronic or mechanical, including photocopying, recording, or by any information storage and retrieval system, without permission in writing from the publisher, except by a reviewer who wishes to quote brief passages in connection with a review written for inclusion in a magazine, newspaper, or broadcast.

For further information:

The Kabbalah Centre
155 E. 48th St., New York, NY 10017
1062 S. Robertson Blvd., Los Angeles, CA 90035

1.800.Kabbalah
www.kabbalah.com

First Edition, April 2006
Printed in Canada
ISBN 1-57189-548-5

Design: Hyun Min Lee

Days of POWER

{ Part Two }

www.kabbalah.com™

R AV   P. S.   B ERG

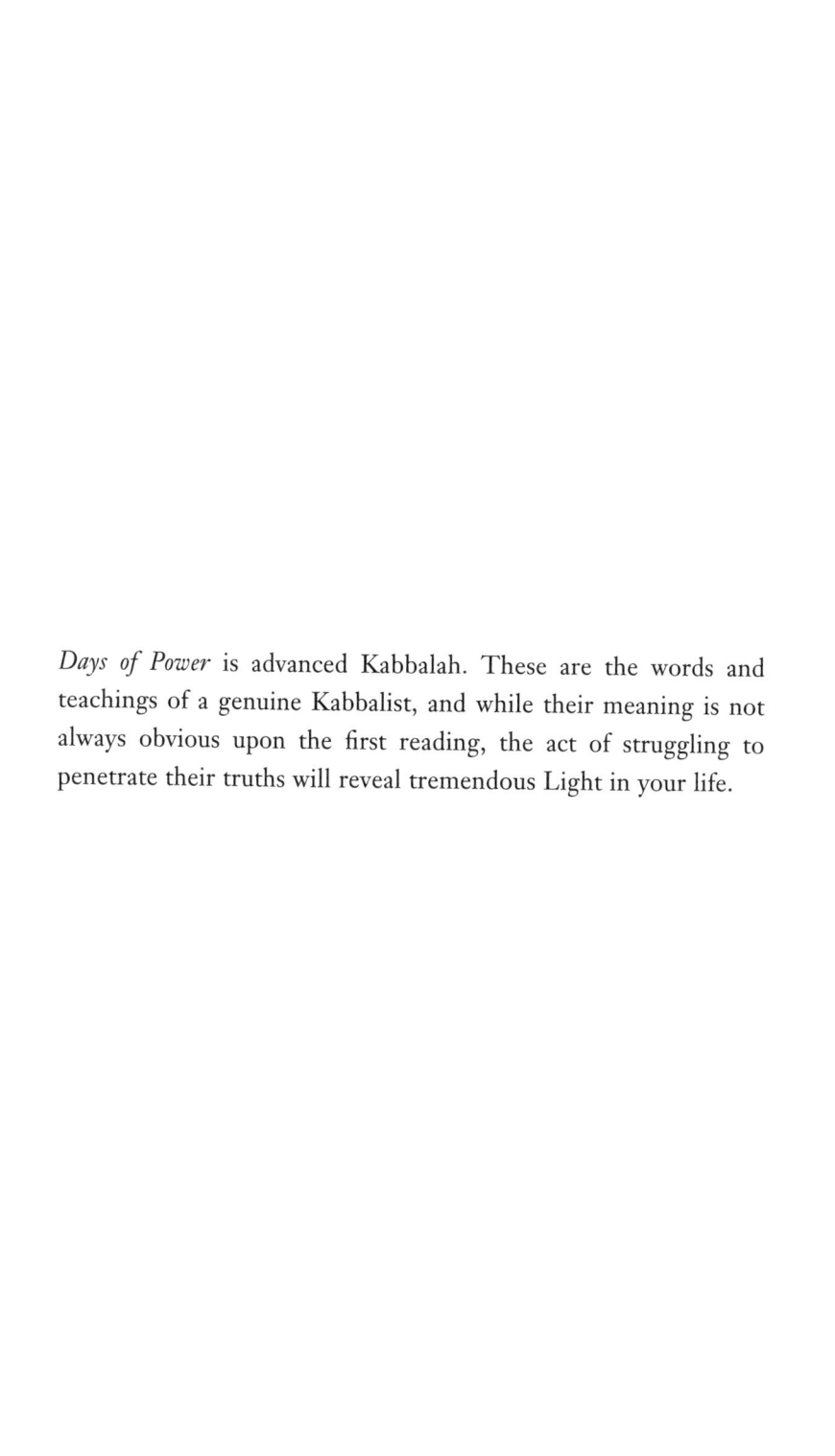

Days of Power is advanced Kabbalah. These are the words and teachings of a genuine Kabbalist, and while their meaning is not always obvious upon the first reading, the act of struggling to penetrate their truths will reveal tremendous Light in your life.

Acknowledgments

For my wife, Karen. In the vastness of cosmic space and the infinity of lifetimes, it is my bliss to be your soul mate and to share a lifetime with you.

Table of CONTENTS

Foreword by Yehuda Berg	xiii
CHANUKAH AND ROSH CHODESH TEVET (CAPRICORN)	1
ROSH CHODESH SHVAT (AQUARIUS)	57
TU BISHVAT (15TH OF AQUARIUS)	69
ROSH CHODESH ADAR (PISCES)	83
THE SEVENTH OF ADAR–THE DEATH ANNIVERSARY OF MOSES	93
PURIM	99
ROSH CHODESH NISSAN (ARIES)	119
PESACH (PASSOVER)	125
Chametz	135
The Seder Plate	137
The Hagaddah	142

Table of Contents

Rosh Chodesh Iyar (Taurus) — 151

Lag B'Omer–Death Anniversary of Rav Shimon Bar Yohai — 161

Rosh Chodesh Sivan (Gemini) — 177

Shavuot — 189

Rosh Chodesh Tammuz (Cancer) — 205

Rosh Chodesh Av (Leo) — 219

The Fifth of Av–The Death Anniversary of Rav Isaac Luria (The Ari) — 227

Tisha B'Av (9th of Leo) — 245

Tu B'Av (15th of Leo) — 255

Appendix

Diagram 1 — 268
Diagram 2 — 269
Diagram 3 — 270
Diagram 4 — 271
Diagram 5 — 272
Daigram 6 — 273

Foreword

The book you are now holding is more than just a mass of pages filled with kabbalistic teachings; it is a spiritual compass. Rav Berg, my father and teacher, created this compass for those of us who are on a spiritual journey—we who are strong enough to forge ourselves a path yet vulnerable enough to ask for help along the way.

The Bible tells us of Moses' unwavering desire to guide the Israelites out of their slavery in Egypt. You will read about that story in this book. Today, few of us live in Egypt, and none of us professes the ability to split the Red Sea. Yet in our time, it has very much been the Rav's mission to guide us out of our own slavery—our bondage to the desire to receive for the self alone. Moses knew he was a leader, but he knew that his mission was not for himself; it was for the people and their connection to the Light force of the Creator. So too does the Rav live every day of his life. Moses knew of the cosmic windows that open to support us in our journey, and within the pages of this book lie those very secrets. As you read these pages, it will be as though you are learning with Moses himself.

Use this book as your guiding light through the days and months of the kabbalistic calendar, and let it guide you to the opportunities and gifts that the Creator has given to us to empower us on our journey. Share the wisdom with others, and pass on the priceless teachings of Moses, as the Rav has passed them to us.

Yehuda Berg

Introduction

The title of this book, *Days of Power*, was chosen very carefully. Over the years, many books have been written about holidays and their spiritual meanings—and virtually all of them, I believe, could have been titled "Days of Memory," or perhaps "Days of Commemoration." The kabbalistic perspective expressed in *Days of Power*, however, is something entirely different from what we're used to. It goes far beyond either secular or conventionally religious interpretations of what holidays really are.

This is a very important point. In the everyday world, our concept of holidays is based on remembering, memorializing, and paying homage to some event in the past. Patriotic holidays such as the Fourth of July or Memorial Day, for example, commemorate the signing of the Declaration of Independence in 1776, and honor the men and women who died in the nation's wars. A traditional understanding of religious holidays follows the same principle: Christmas is the birthday of Jesus Christ; Passover is a remembrance of the Israelites' escape from Egyptian bondage; and Purim is the anniversary of their salvation from a genocidal plot. And certain holidays, of course, are simply a recognition of turning-point moments in the calendar, such as the New Year celebration of *Rosh Hashanah*.

Kabbalah, however, absolutely and completely rejects remembrance or recognition as the basis of holidays. In place of commemoration, a kabbalist focuses on *connection*—that is, the opportunity to tap into the unique energies that exist at the specific points in time that we call holidays. With this is mind, the meaning of the title *Days of Power* becomes clear. The holidays are literally power sources that we can access using the teachings and tools of Kabbalah. Those tools include prayers, ceremonies, *The Bible*, *The Zohar*, and continuing study and understanding of what God really intends for us—which is, by the way, nothing less than complete happiness and total freedom from any form of unhappiness, including death itself.

The concept of holidays as Days of Power—as points of potential connection with specific forms of energy—is the key premise of this book. In addition to this, several other fundamental concepts need to be clarified here at the start.

Most readers will notice, for example, that the holidays discussed in *Days of Power* are the holidays normally considered

"Jewish holidays." Yet that phrase appears nowhere in these pages. In fact, I have made a focused effort to make it clear that these holidays, like all the tools and teachings of Kabbalah, belong to all of humankind. Just as no one would say that the energy of gravity is a Jewish force, the energies of the various holidays are neither Jewish, Christian, Buddhist, or Hindu. They are simply basic aspects of the way the universe works, and they are beyond identification with any nation or religion.

In order to make the distinction between conventional Judaism and Kabbalah as clear and consistent as possible, I've also used terms such as "Israelite" and "people of Israel" throughout these pages. Occasionally, the term "chosen people" does occur in connection with the Israelites, but it's very important to understand exactly what this means. It does not mean a nationality. Kabbalah teaches that the people of Israel are those human beings who, at Mount Sinai, received the infinitely powerful package of energy called the *Torah*. They chose to accept the spiritual system. And, as always in Kabbalah, this was not a moment in ancient history but rather an event that each of us can and should reprise in our own lives. In this sense, everyone who accepts the tools and teachings of Kabbalah that God intends for us is an Israelite. But that's not all: Every Israelite also accepts the responsibility of sharing those tools and teachings. This is the real meaning of "chosen people:" It is not that the people have *been* chosen; it is that the people *have* chosen.

You, no matter who you are, can make that choice right now. This is totally unrelated to the religion in which you were raised, or the country where you were born, or any other fact about you. To explain this, I often use the metaphor of turning on a light switch to banish darkness from a dark room. Anyone can turn on the light. The electricity doesn't know or care about the details of your identity. What's more, you don't need to understand physics or electrical engineering in order to flip the switch or to benefit from that action. Increased knowledge can enhance your appreciation of what takes place, but that's yet to come. The all-important first step is simply understanding that the opportunities described in this book are not just available to you, but divinely intended for you. The rest is between you and that metaphorical light switch.

One final point. As I've said, Kabbalah is not religion, and to make that clear I've avoided using words that have clear religious associations. But the ultimate religious word, God, does appear many times in *Days of Power*. Although God is spoken of in human terms throughout the biblical narrative or in the commentaries on *The Bible*, Kabbalah definitely does not understand God as a man on a cloud, a woman riding in a chariot, or any other anthropomorphic form. This is made very clear in *The Bible*'s original Hebrew, where the word "God" is designated by a number of different words, including "*Adonai*," "*Elohim*," and *Hashem*." Each of these words expresses a different aspect of God—a different energy. Sometimes this energy is one of mercy and forgiveness; at other points in *The Bible*, there is anger and severity.

But here is the key kabbalistic point: it is *we ourselves* who determine how the energy flows down. To understand this, consider the fact that electricity is always present in the wiring of a house. If a person recklessly chooses to put his finger in a wall socket, he will get a shock—the cause of which was his own action. On the other hand, if the same person plugs a toaster in the wall socket, he will get a piece of toast. In both cases, it would be foolish to "blame" or "credit" the nature of electricity for the consequence of the actions. Like electricity, gravity, or even nuclear energy, the power of the Creator is infinite, unlimited potential. How will that potential manifest itself? We ourselves make that decision in every moment of our lives.

Always and forever, God gives us the effect we need based on the cause we have set in motion. If we need God's presence in a certain form of energy, it is the nature of God to fulfill that need. But the ultimate purpose always remains the same: to move us toward total freedom from chaos, pain, illness, and death.

That is the purpose of the holidays, and it is also the intention of this book. May *Days of Power* help bring you the joy and fulfillment that are your true destiny.

Chanukah and Rosh Chodesh Tevet
(CAPRICORN)

Traditionally, *Chanukah* is considered a joyous and festive holiday—one whose focus has become the exchanging of gifts. The term *tradition*, however, does not even exist in the kabbalistic lexicon. Indeed, the traditional approach practiced by members of all faiths has caused most people in the world to abandon religion outright. *Chanukah* in particular is almost meaningless for most Israelites in the world today. Were it not for the jelly doughnuts and gifts with which *Chanukah* has become associated, it is doubtful that anyone would even remember to celebrate this holiday.

Those who are somewhat familiar with *Chanukah* might know it as the Festival of Lights וג האורים *(Chag Ha'urim)*. The name *Chag Ha'urim* is the result of an historic event. Kabbalistically, however, the word חג *(chag)* means "moves in a circle"—that is, "forms a connection with the infinite Light"—and there is no relation between *chag* חַג and *chagigah* חֲגִיגָה (celebration), or festival. Indeed, the term festival is a completely distorted translation of the original term. Moreover, the long-held practice of placing the *Chanukiah* (*Chanukah* menorah or candelabra) on the windowsill to "publicize the miracle" is nowhere near the sages' original intention, which was in fact based on Kabbalah—and the custom of exchanging gifts among family members is more likely connected to Christmas than to *Chanukah*. This is so for two reasons: First, the act of sharing and caring for others is supposed to be maintained throughout the year, not just during a particular holiday. Second, because giving within the family circle is akin to giving to ourselves, it does not truly constitute sharing. Gift giving is associated with the holiday of *Purim*, not *Chanukah*; indeed, the idea on *Purim* is to exchange presents outside the family circle rather than within it—to help care for the needy and less fortunate.

When the Greeks ruled the land, they forbade the Israelites to study spirituality; they desecrated the Holy Temple and defiled the oil that was used to light the menorah. The *Maccabim* defeated the Greeks on *Chanukah*. On the 25th day of *Kislev* (Sagittarius), the prolonged war reached a sudden end with the victory of the *Maccabim*. Following this victory, the Greek empire began to disintegrate throughout the world, including places whose inhabitants had not intended to rebel. On that day, while conducting a search throughout the Temple, the *Chashmona'im* found a single vial that still carried the seal of the High Priest. This small vial contained exceptionally pure oil that was charged with special consciousness, as explained in the Torah in the Books of Exodus and Leviticus. Using this oil, the *Chashmona'im* lit the extinguished menorah to announce their victory, and the oil that flowed from the small vial, which was supposed to last for only one day, burned for eight. This is the historic event that traditionalists cite as grounds for *Chanukah* to be called the Festival of Lights. Nevertheless, the *"Al Hanisim"* (miracles section of the prayer book), which is read during the holidays of *Chanukah* and *Purim*, offers no hint of this brilliant military victory. Instead, it explains that the victory resulted only from the total support of the Creator that was revealed on that day—much like the miracle of the Exodus from Egypt, when the Creator took the Israelites and led them out of Egypt. The defeat of the Greeks was not a result of the military power of the Israelites, but rather a result of the revelation of the Creator's power—a burst of Light that freed the Israelites from the Greeks' oppression on this day of all days.

If this is so, however, what is the correct way to celebrate the holiday? And what, in addition to the victory, are we celebrating? Ordinarily we do not recall experiences from previous incarnations, and most of us might not have been in Israel—or even in the world—during the Revolt of the *Maccabim*. Therefore, how are we to know what really took place in Israel at that time and how *Chanukah* should be celebrated? In *Sha'ar Hakavanot—Gates of Meditation*, Rav Isaac Luria, The Ari, reveals the answers to these and other questions.

According to the *Talmud*, the *Cohanim* (priests) of the *Chashmona'i* family led the revolt. Such a phenomenon has never been mentioned before in the history of the Israelites; indeed, no case is mentioned in the Torah in which *Cohanim* stood at the head of the army. The *Cohanim* were always in the Temple and did not leave it for any other activity. This special historical detail hints at what occurred during *Chanukah*. Contrary to common belief, the reason the Land of Israel is called the Holy Land and Jerusalem the Holy City is that Jerusalem was originally holy in itself, which is why the Temple was located there; it did not become holy as a result of the building of the Temple. The Land of Israel is the cause, and the Temple is the result.

Chanukah is mentioned in the Torah in a concealed manner. All festivals, or *mo'adim* מוֹעֲדִים, that are mentioned in the Torah are cosmic events—which is to say that on these *mo'adim*, the Gates of Heaven open up. But what does this mean? Does it imply that the Gates of Heaven remain locked on all other days of the year? Specifically, *mo'adim* are the days on which we are given the opportunity to connect to certain energies that flow out of the upper worlds. *Chanukah*, *Pesach*, *Rosh Hashanah*, and *Sukkot* are not year-round holidays; they are events that assist us in the injection of energy, and that is why we are so happy when they arrive. Our exposure to these energies is similar to the retracting headlights of a car: We push a button, the headlights pop up, and the light shines out. At all other times, the headlights are covered and therefore do not give light.

But why is the spiritual Light of the holidays not revealed on all other days of the year? *The Zohar* and The Ari explain that one must always recognize the *klipot* (spiritual shells), which exist in the world to enable us to remove Bread of Shame. In effect, the Creator pitted the pure system and the impure system against one another so that true freedom of choice might be practiced. Were it not for the *klipot*, all of us would be good all the time, and there would then be no possibility of removing Bread of Shame. At the same time, we do not wish to strengthen and nourish the *klipot* more than is necessary for their actual existence. If the Light of the holidays were exposed throughout the entire year with no restriction, the *klipot* would incessantly feed off it, and that is something we do not want. Therefore, the Light is revealed only for restricted, measured periods of time.

We know that no holiday is celebrated in remembrance of a specific physical or historical event. Therefore, we ask, Why was the oil jar discovered on the 25th day of the lunar month of *Kislev*, which falls in the same period as December? Why did the *Chashmona'im* defeat the Greeks on the 25th day of *Kislev*? Let us go to the root, to the source, to investigate and seek out the spiritual reason that brought about the historic events related to this holiday.

Since *Chanukah* is a holiday, it should immediately be obvious that a cosmic event occurred on the 25th day of *Kislev*, the result of which was the victory of the *Maccabim* over the Greeks. Therefore, it is not the victory we are celebrating but rather the cosmic event that takes place throughout the universe each *Chanukah*. To be sure, many cosmic events influence our lives: Tides are a result of the effect of the moon on earth, and our characteristics and ways of life are influenced by the 12 signs of the zodiac, the moon, and the planets of our solar system. In much the same way, the Torah explains that *Pesach* (Passover) and other holidays mark cosmic influences. We do not celebrate any holiday simply for religious reasons because, according to Kabbalah, the Torah is not a religion.

These holidays were intended to supply us with knowledge regarding the cosmic time schedule and the opportunities we have to connect to the cosmic reservoir of energy. Whenever we feel weak and wish to strengthen ourselves, we eat something, go to a doctor, or read a book—but none of these solutions truly protects us from negative energy. Listening to music may temporarily improve our mood, but it cannot thwart an intrusion into our home or deliver us from accidents and disease. There is no physical solution that offers a comprehensive, balanced response to all the problems and challenges that life places before us. *Chanukah*, as mentioned earlier, is not a holiday that is meant to mark a military victory; nor was it intended for the distribution of presents to family members or for playing with *dreidels* (spinning tops) and eating *latkes* (potato pancakes). Instead, this holiday was intended to supply the answer to all of life's problems. In short, the Festival of *Chanukah* enables us to connect to the cosmic reservoir of the energy of life, health, success, safety, and continuity.

But if we are given the opportunity to connect to the Light on the holidays, what prevents the *klipot* from taking advantage of that opportunity? In *The Zohar*, Rav Shimon Bar Yochai explains that when the Light is revealed on the holidays, it is revealed indirectly, in an encrypted manner, so that only by means of meditation and special actions can we connect to it. This is the reason Rav Shimon came into the world and taught the special intentions, which The Ari later explained in greater detail. These meditations are known only to those who have studied Kabbalah, and the knowledge they contain appeared in the universe only in Aramaic. As a result, Satan is not familiar with the meditations and cannot take advantage of the Light that is revealed on holidays and festivals. For the same reason, says Rav Shimon, there is no chance of bringing about redemption if Kabbalah is not studied and the knowledge that *The Zohar* embodies is not applied.

Within all knowledge there is encoded energy. We feel the energy in the knowledge and aspire to connect to it. As long as the message embodied in that knowledge remains encoded, however, we cannot do so, and frustration results. But after investing an effort in studying, deciphering the code, and connecting to the Light, we can enjoy the fulfillment that the Light gives us—a feeling of joy and satisfaction. As Rav Shimon explains, however, it is not merely the Light of the holidays that is encoded, but the entire Torah as well. Each letter is a channel for energy. Therefore, without the wisdom of Kabbalah, we have no possibility of connecting to the Light of the Torah. It must be understood that this has nothing to do with what took place during the time of the Temple and the Greeks, which is just a scrap of information that, while teaching us how to be victorious, does not assist us with our lives today.

Why do we celebrate *Chanukah* even though it is not specifically mentioned in the Torah? Is it because of the miracle that took place on those days? Many great miracles have occurred in the course of history, but we do not mark each of them with a special holiday. *Purim* is not explicitly mentioned in the Torah, but we nonetheless celebrate it each year. According to tradition, on *Purim* we celebrate a miracle that took place during the reign of the Persian empire. Why of all miracles do these two receive note each year?

Have you ever wondered about the date on which the *Chashmona'im* achieved victory, bringing the prolonged war against the Greeks to a sudden halt? Since the answer is found in the Torah's cosmic code, we must seek the answer in the universe. The cosmic event that brought victory to the *Chashmona'im* occurred in the month of *Kislev*, which corresponds to the sign of Sagittarius. Therefore, Sagittarius influenced these events and is related to their cause. In addition to this heavenly script, we must also discuss an even more important factor: Jupiter, the ruling planet of the sign of Sagittarius. The signs of the zodiac are channels through which the planets affect our lives. The victory of the *Chashmona'im* and the miracle of the oil container may thus be understood by shedding light on the planet Jupiter and its zodiac sign.

The word קֶשֶׁת *keshet*, (meaning archery bow or rainbow), which describes the sign of Sagittarius and enables us to connect to the power revealed in the universe during the month of *Kislev*, refers not only to an ancient weapon—the bow and arrow—but also to a rainbow and the combination of energies that the rainbow contains: right, left, and central (white, red, and green). Without delving into a detailed explanation of the relationship between the three columns and the proton, electron, and neutron, the word keshet implies that something that occurs under this sign imbues the universe with the force of unity expressed in an atom. All those who know how to connect to this force can harness it during the month of *Kislev*. There is no source of nuclear energy in the world more powerful than the atom. This energy is based on the balance and unity that exist between the proton—an expression of the desire to share; the electron—an expression of the desire to receive; and the neutron—an expression of the balance between the two, the central column.

It is no accident that the sign of Sagittarius belongs to the third month after *Rosh Hashanah*. The months of the year are divided into four groups of three months each. Sagittarius is the third in its group and is preceded by Libra and Scorpio, and its position hints at the nature of its internal consciousness. The rainbow contains within it symmetry, centralization, and the balance of right, left, and central columns; this is the consciousness that brought about the expression of the energy of Jupiter. The *Chashmona'im* knew how to harness this energy, and that is how they defeated the

Greeks and performed the miracle of *Chanukah*. It should now be obvious that we are not discussing an Israelite tradition but rather a lesson—one that enables us to connect to the same immense power that brought a world empire to its knees on the 25th of *Kislev*.

At the same time, additional questions must be posed. For example, if the immense power of nuclear energy is available to us throughout the entire month of *Kislev*, why did the great victory take place on the 25th day of the month? In the *Sefer Yetzirah—The Book of Formation*, written by Abraham the Patriarch—it is stated that the power of the Aramaic alphabet lies in the fact that all planets, all kinds of energy intelligences, and all signs of the zodiac were created by the letters of the Aramaic alphabet. The 22 letters are responsible for the three columns (right, left, and central), the seven planets, and the 12 signs of the Zodiac: 3 + 7 + 12 = 22 in total. *The Book of Formation* further supplies us with the cosmic information by means of which we can connect to this energy. Abraham stated that Jupiter was created using the letter ג (*Gimel*). The numerical value of *Gimel* is three. Sagittarius and the month of *Kislev* were created using the letter ס (*Samech*). The numerical value of *Samech* is 60, and 60 + 3 = 63. The same number, 63, is related to the *Sfirah* (level) of *Binah*.

But why do we celebrate the miracles of *Chanukah* and *Purim* and not other, no less impressive miracles? When we walk in the footsteps of the sages and examine the meaning of *Chanukah* from a kabbalistic perspective—the month's zodiac sign, its planet, its letters, the names related to the holiday, and the duration of the holiday—we reach the conclusion that we are dealing with a cosmic event that is encrypted in the Torah. If this is the case, however, what is the difference between those holidays which are explicitly mentioned in the Torah and the two that are not mentioned, *Chanukah* and *Purim*? Incidentally, *Purim*, which is celebrated in the month of *Adar*, is ruled by Jupiter as well. It is an interesting coincidence that the victory over the Greeks on *Chanukah* and the victory over the Persians on *Purim* both occurred under the rule of the same planet. What is unique about these two dates? What is transmitted through the universe that justifies treating these two cases in a manner identical to that of other festivals explicitly described in the Torah? And why call them holidays at all? Perhaps it would be better to call them days of wholeness—days of holiness, of continuity, of everlastingness, of infinite cyclic flowing.

According to the story, the miracle of *Chanukah* represents the military victory of the *Maccabim* over the Greek army and the amount of oil that would ordinarily burn only a single day lasting for eight days. But why do we not celebrate more impressive miracles, such as the parting of the Red Sea or the conquering of Jericho? What connection between the adventures of the *Maccabim* and our lives today justifies our celebration of these events? As is widely known, we do not have customs without a reason. Each and every act we perform in the course of our holidays and festivals is intended to help us connect to the energies being transmitted throughout the universe at that time, such that we may use those energies to solve our problems and improve the quality of our lives. If we examine the miracle of the oil in a logical manner, we can say that since the oil lasted eight days and should ordinarily have lasted only one, the miracle began only on the second day. Yet if that is the case, we should celebrate the holiday for only seven days. From a kabbalistic perspective, however, it is more important to ask about the source of power that caused the oil to last exactly eight days rather than fourteen, five, or four—and the answer is not "because that's what happened," as physicists would reply. Effects can never be causes. Causes are found in the spiritual realm; results exist in the physical realm. Therefore, a physical event such as the miracle of the oil jar or the military victory of the *Maccabim*, which is necessarily a result, can never serve as a fundamental cause of any matter. When a kabbalist investigates reality, he is not satisfied with a mere description of that reality but is interested in understanding, in the most thorough way possible, its underlying rules and laws.

If we count the *Sfirot* of the Tree of Life in a downward direction, from *Keter* to *Malchut*, we will find that *Hod* is the eighth *Sfirah* *Sfirot* of the Tree of Life in an upward direction, from *Malchut* to *Keter*, we will find that *Binah* is the eighth *Sfirah* (see Diagrams 1 & 2). On *Chanukah*, a great Light is revealed that is connected to these two *Sfirot*. In addition, reciprocal relations are expressed between Lights and vessels in the realm of the bottom eight *Sfirot*, which are revealed by these two methods of counting. Although these Lights and vessels have existed since Creation, they were first revealed and realized thanks to the *Maccabim*, who, by virtue of their unity, rose from *Malchut* to *Zeir Anpin* (Diagram 3) (a combination of *Chesed* through to *Yesod*). We are celebrating the miracle of the flight of the *Maccabim* from the world of *Malchut*, against nature, to *Zeir Anpin*. The military victory of the *Maccabim* and the miracle of the oil were only results of the Maccabean transcendence. The power of *Binah* and *Hod*, discovered by the *Maccabim*, could have caused the oil to last for any length of time. Mattityahu, the high priest and father of the *Maccabim*, chose to light the menorah for exactly eight days in order to indicate to us the true source of the victory: the Creator's power of Light, which is revealed through the *Sfirah* of *Binah* in *Netzach*, *Hod*, and *Yesod* (Diagram 4). Mattityahu reveals to us that miracles can happen in each succeeding generation if we connect to this force, just as he himself did. Incidentally, *Sukkot* lasts for eight days as well. The concept of eight days is neither unusual nor strange. The departure from the framework of the seven lower *Sfirot* once again connects us to the *Sfirah* of *Binah*, the cosmic energy reservoir. This is the consciousness of an eight-day holiday.

We light the *Chanukiah* not in memory of the miraculous events, which are a result, but rather to connect to the cause. The meditations for lighting the *Chanukiah* connect directly to the Light of the *Sfirah* of *Hod*. The miracle of the oil jar was created by Mattityahu, who rose above the nature of physical reality and changed that nature. The reason the *Maccabim*—the members of the family of priesthood—found the sealed oil jar is, in fact, the essence of the holiday. The finding of the oil could never constitute a reason for a holiday, for oil is a physical thing. But why was the oil found? And how does one define a miracle? A miracle is any event that does not follow the course of nature. Anything that lies beyond nature as it is known to us is a miracle. Anything supernatural is a cosmic phenomenon. The greatest power used to remove chaos is embodied in the Hebrew word נס nes, (or miracle). What do physicians, scientists, and all other people say each time chaos infiltrates our lives? "In this situation, only a miracle could save us." What they mean to say is that only a miracle can turn chaos into Light, thereby restoring order and harmony.

All who have read the chapters dealing with *Rosh Hashanah* and *Yom Kippur*, in *Days of Power Volume One* know that *Binah* is the energy reservoir that nourishes us during *Tishrei* (Libra), the month that corresponds to October. We connect to this energy reservoir in order to receive enough life to last us the whole year. These holidays occur when the planets and constellations give the world the abundance of life energy required by all its inhabitants for an additional year. The Torah states that human beings throughout the world are judged on *Rosh Hashanah*; if they wish to do something about it, they would be best off connecting to *Binah* and drawing its energy into their lives. The Torah dictates to us the prescription for success, which lies in the *Shofar* and all the other details of the procedure. The same holds true for *Yom Kippur* and *Sukkot*. The Torah's purpose is to teach us what to do for our own good so that we may gain another year of quality life.

On *Hoshana Rabba*, the portion of energy that each person on earth has received for the New Year during the month of *Tishrei* is sealed and implemented. At the same time, on the 25th day of *Kislev*, the latecomers are given another chance to connect to *Binah* and to attract additional life energy. Therefore, the Festival of *Chanukah* is connected to the events of the month of *Tishrei* and has direct implications for life expectancy and quality. An additional hint to the holiday riddle lies in the full name of the revolt's leader: Mattityahu, *Cohen Gadol Chashmona'i* (High Priest). How did it happen that this man was personally responsible for the fall of the Greek empire? We do not accept "just because" as a satisfactory answer. We know, for example, that the name מ‎שֶׁ‎ה Moshe (Moses) derives its strength from the combination מ‎ה‎שׁ of the 72 Names, which allows for a connection to the cosmic power of healing. This is the secret of the power of Moses, the Patriarch. In a similar manner, a deep meaning is imbued in each name and word connected to every holiday and festival we celebrate. The numerical value of the word מ‎ת‎ת‎י‎ה‎ו (Mattityahu) is equal to that of ר‎אשׁ ה‎שׁ‎נ‎ה (*Rosh Hashanah*)—861. As Shakespeare said: "A rose is a rose. A rose by any other name could seemingly be called by any other name, but it is not. A rose emits a characteristic scent and is called by this name because its essence is such and not otherwise. If it were called by a different name, it would not emit the scent of a rose." Thus, in the name Mattityahu, the eight days of the holiday and the number 63 join together in a common solution to the holiday's crossword puzzle.

In short, *Chanukah* is not a holiday we must celebrate in the name of tradition. Should it continue to be presented in this way, we can rest assured that within a matter of years no one will be familiar with it anymore, just as many other religious traditions in the world have lost their meaning. In the Age of Aquarius, people no longer follow leaders in a blind, robotic fashion; instead, they do so out of consciousness, wisdom, and free choice. When the sages investigated the reasons for celebrating the Festival of *Chanukah*, they concluded that the issue pertained not to an additional miracle, but rather to a cosmic event that essentially re-created that of *Rosh Hashanah*. We thus celebrate neither the miracle of the oil jar nor the victory over the Greeks, but rather the connection to the *Sfirah* of *Binah* and to the consciousness of *Zeir Anpin*—the desire to share. The sages tell us that *Chanukah* is like a small *Rosh Hashanah*—and as you know, *Rosh Hashanah* is meant for all human beings, all religions, and people at all levels of consciousness: both those who know how to connect to the Light and those who do not. But those who do know can choose freely and control their own fate, whereas those who do not know are destined to be slaves to the deceptions of fate. By applying the wisdom of Kabbalah, we are able to harness the forces of the universe that are revealed on these holidays, and through them improve our physical and spiritual state of existence. This is not religiosity; this is logic.

Who does not want to improve his or her life? *Chanukah* and *Rosh Hashanah* are similar in that both holidays give us an opportunity to connect to a force that strengthens our physical and spiritual DNA as well as that of the world around us. Environmental DNA is the code that governs our relationship with the world around us—other human beings, the weather, the forces of nature, traffic, and so on.

In the month of *Kislev* (Sagittarius), which corresponds to the month of December, we are given an opportunity to increase the life force at our disposal. If during the month of *Tishrei* (Libra), which corresponds to October, we receive a portion of life that will last us less than an entire year—say, only until February, March, June, or July—on *Chanukah* we may again connect to *Binah* and draw the energy we lack so that we may safely reach the next *Rosh Hashanah*. This is truly the resurrection of the dead, although it occurs before death actually takes place. *Chanukah* is Mattityahu's time—the time of 861, when *Rosh Hashanah* returns to visit us and *Shemini Atzeret* comes back to see us. All those who were sentenced not to arrive safely and soundly at next year's *Rosh Hashanah* can, on *Chanukah*, complete that which is lacking.

Sukkot is another holiday that, rather than commemorating an historic event, affords us an opportunity to build a vessel and a spiritual protective system. On *Sukkot*, we do not celebrate the wanderings of the Israelites in the desert; nor do we celebrate their having lived in temporary structures for 40 years. Our goal is not to teach the rich to remember the less fortunate who are living in ramshackle dwellings. After all, how useful can it be for us to address a socioeconomic issue by living in a sparse booth for a week at the beginning of each winter? Naturally, this is not the case. Instead, the

Succah is nothing more than a channel whose purpose and properties are specified in the *Days of Power Volume One* that deals with the Festival of *Sukkot*. Like *Sukkot*, *Chanukah* lasts eight days. On both of these holidays, we are given an opportunity to obtain life that will last us from this moment until the next *Rosh Hashanah*. In effect, the *Tishrei* holidays enable us to connect and draw life for the coming year. Therefore, if we have connected properly, the *Tishrei* holidays will supply us with the personal and environmental DNA we need for an entire year. There is no religious observance involved here; only a means of improving the quality of our lives. And this implies that we must function under several conditions, among which are caring for others, sharing, and the like. Yet these facets do not explain the full significance of *Chanukah*. As is the case with *Sukkot*, all we have to do to connect to the energy of *Chanukah* is know that the transmission is taking place in the universe. Those who do not know cannot connect.

Nowadays, one can readily buy electric menorahs that can be used in place of wax candles or oil and wicks. Indeed, many rabbis are of the opinion that lighting an electric *Chanukiah* will by itself permit us to fulfill the obligation involved in maintaining the tradition of *Chanukah*. But it is not sufficient to execute the communication with *Binah* with the consciousness of the desire to share! The Light of *Chasadim* (mercy) is what we seek on *Sukkot* and on *Chanukah*. During *Chanukah*, as with *Sukkot*, many accessories are at our disposal for the purpose of realizing the communication. Lighting the *Chanukiah* without the correct meditations does not ensure a connection to the cosmic reservoir of energy; to the contrary, it guarantees a high probability of a lack of connection to the special event that occurs only when the planet Jupiter and the constellation of Sagittarius cooperate. The significance of the candles, or the oil wicks, lies in the fact that they are a means of attracting the Light of *Binah* directly to us. By means of this Light, we are able to defeat any enemy and win any battle while sitting at home, even though the physical battle might be far from our place of rest. That is how Mattityahu affected the entire Greek empire without leaving his son Yehuda and without sending messengers to other lands. The influence that spiritual power wields on the universe can remove negativity from its source, no matter where that source may be. This, in effect, is what happened on *Chanukah*. The *Chasmona'im* knew it and connected to the reservoir of cosmic energy. The oil jar was found, and it lasted for eight days because of a cosmic event called Little *Sukkot*, which delegated an immense energetic abundance onto us. This is what we celebrate, and nothing else. The military victory was only a result of this cosmic revelation. According to the *Siddur* (daily connection book), from the moment the great Light was revealed, all subsequent events occurred of their own accord: the military victory, the purification of the Temple, and the lighting of the *Chanukiah*.

Although we connect to *Binah* during the *Tishrei* holidays, on *Chanukah* we connect to *Binah* on a more physical level, in the framework of *Netzach*, *Hod*, and *Yesod*—that is to say, *Binah* of *Netzach*, *Binah* of *Hod*, and *Binah* of *Yesod* (Diagram 4). It is as though *Tishrei* gave us access to the main energy warehouse, whereas on *Chanukah* we are afforded entry into the small storeroom of a local supermarket branch. Indeed, the local branch is more convenient than the main warehouse, but its inherent potential is more defined and limited. The issue of accessibility is amply demonstrated in the fact that in order to reach *Binah* on *Yom Kippur* we must go to synagogue, whereas on *Chanukah* the communication required to connect to *Binah* in *Netzach*, in *Hod*, and in *Yesod* may be performed in our own homes, without even a *minyan* (a quorum of ten men required for total energy tapping during a prayer service). The communication is so easy that it is not necessary to fast, and there is not even a *Megilah* or scroll to read, as there is on *Purim*. By following the five precepts in conjunction with the energy of the day, we disconnect ourselves from *Malchut* on *Yom Kippur* and rise to a place that is free of *klipot*, to levels in which Satan has no bearing. On *Chanukah* we are on lower strata, and all that is required of us is knowledge of the address: *Binah* of *Netzach*, *Binah* of *Hod*, and *Binah* of *Yesod*.

On *Pesach* we celebrate a truly great event: the transition from slavery to freedom. But the Torah is full of evidence that the Israelites did not even intend to leave Egypt. In fact, on many occasions they expressed an explicit desire to return to Egypt, to the steak, cucumbers, and onions. *The Zohar* and the *Talmud* note with regret that had the Creator not forced the Exodus from Egypt on the people of Israel, they would forever have remained slaves to the desire to receive for the self alone, because the members of that generation were the least spiritual ever to have lived. The

Israelites initiated neither the Exodus from Egypt nor the revelation of the power that caused it. This was an initiative that originated in the upper worlds alone.

Let us now look at another holiday mentioned in the Torah: the Revelation at Mount Sinai, which is considered to be the greatest event in the history of the world since Creation itself. On this occasion, the document according to which members of all religions live—or that which at least serves as the basis of all religions—was revealed. Did the Israelites long for the revelation of the Creator and the Torah? Indeed, these people had no intention of receiving laws and judgments that would restrict their desire to receive for themselves alone. The *Talmud* states that the Creator uprooted Mount Sinai, positioned the Israelites in the crater where the mountain once stood, and said to them, "Either you receive the Torah, or here will be your place of burial, for there is no sense in continuing your existence on earth. What will eventually happen, if you do not accept the Torah, is that each and every one of you will eat the other alive. In other words, life on earth will disappear in a global war." It can thus be seen that both *Pesach* and *Shavuot* were meant not for the Israelites of that generation but rather for generations to come—for the future. In fact, it might be said that the Israelite people of that era totally failed, for immediately after having received the Torah, they built the Golden Calf. The only significance in commemorating the event lies in the fact that in each and every generation, the same revelation occurs—the same cosmic event. If the members of the Exodus generation were not wise enough to connect to the event, we are not prevented from doing so today. In both cases we see that the Creator initiated an event, and the Israelite people were forced to cooperate.

The first time we are informed that the Israelites acted according to the precepts of the Torah—creating balance, symmetry, and harmony and bringing peace and love to the world—was on *Chanukah*. The Greeks ordered the Israelites to stop studying the Torah and to go back to idolatry. The essential difference between idolatry and the belief in a single God, which was introduced into the world by Abraham the Patriarch, is that the single God represents the desire to share. Belief in this God teaches us to share from with in— that is to say, to supplant the desire to receive for the self alone with the desire to receive for the sake of sharing. By contrast, idolatry bolsters the desire to receive for the self alone, fostering separation, fragmentation, and death. Therefore, when the Israelite people decided that they were not willing to return to such a consciousness and were unwilling to repeat the mistake of their ancestors in Egypt, they caused the fall of the Greek empire on the 25th day of *Kislev*—for on that day, the energy reservoir of *Binah* reopened, just as it does during the month of *Tishrei*. The combination of Jupiter and Sagittarius—63, opened the energy reservoir door to a handful of Israelites, enabling them to use this energy to bring about the sudden fall of the Greek empire not only in the Land of Israel but throughout the world as well. It is strange, for the members of all other nations conquered by the Greeks did not rebel at all. But by propagating to others the consciousness of the desire to share, the desire to receive for the self alone was forced to surrender.

Despite the death penalty that the Greeks imposed on anyone who studied Torah, the Israelites presented against them the power of the central column, the rainbow. This was the same rainbow that the Creator showed Noah—a sign of complete perfection, a sign of peace, and a guarantee that never again would a deluge destroy the world. As it is known, the rainbow represents the balance and unity of the three columns as expressed within each atom. This power of the central column and the use of it against negative forces, which constitutes the application of the force of resistance, was made by the Israelite people for the first time on *Chanukah*. This did not take place on *Pesach* during the Exodus from Egypt, nor did it occur on *Shavuot* at Mount Sinai or even on *Sukkot*. The first time the Israelites actually lived in the Light of the Torah as a nation rather than as a chosen few—thereby actively bringing about a miracle—was on *Chanukah*. And therein lies the unique quality of this miracle as opposed to other miracles to which the Israelite people have borne witness over the past 2,000 years: The Light and order revealed in the world as a result of this action cleansed the world of all negativity, as represented by the Greek empire—especially the idolatry that embodied the desire to receive for the self alone. Thus, it was not merely a local victory but a global one as well: a triumph of good over evil.

The burning of the *menorah* for eight days is nothing but a sign, a statement, that once again the Light of *Sukkot* has been revealed. When the sages saw Mattityahu, whose name in kabbalistic numerology equals 861, they saw *Rosh Hashanah*—the additional chance at life that human beings receive. In order to arrive at these revelations and understandings, however, evidence was required. This evidence comprised the miracle of the oil jar, Mattityahu's name, the month of *Kislev*, and the other factors we have enumerated. The reason for celebration on *Chanukah* thus resides in the cosmic event that occurs on the 25th day of *Kislev*: the opportunity to reconstruct the *Tishrei* holidays, not the military victory over the Greeks or the miracle of the oil jar. The significance of this miracle lies in the fact that it was the first to have resulted from the Israelites' having performed the Torah's mitzvot, or positive actions, in a collective fashion as a nation rather than as individuals.

This is another factor shared by *Chanukah* and *Purim*. The Miracle of *Purim* occurred following the revelation of tremendous Light that resulted when the Israelite people acted in unison in accordance with the Torah. This revelation of Light caused the Persian empire to fall at a time when it dominated the entire civilized world. Esther and Mordechai recognized that Jupiter enables miracles not only through the cosmic window of Sagittarius but through Pisces as well: the combination of Jupiter and the month of *Adar* (Pisces). The month of March affords access to great intensities of cosmic energy that are transmitted to the earth at this time. *Purim* itself was not the important event but only the signal—an indication of the opportunity to connect to cosmic power. The customs we observe on *Chanukah* can thus be seen not as a religious tradition, but rather as the recipe for connecting to the energy that is transmitted in the universe at that time each year. This is our opportunity to complete the energy we are lacking. That is why we light the candles, and that is why *Chanukah* is called the Festival of Lights: The Light demonstrates an aspect that does not exist in any other physical entity—the aspect of sharing.

Many customs and legends surround *Chanukah*. But the significance of this holiday, as opposed to its Christian counterpart of Christmas, does not lie in the familial and social aspect of the gathering itself or in the exchange of gifts, as we have seen in recent years. In fact, the only holiday on which gift giving is mentioned as a *mitzvah* is *Purim*. Since most people have lost contact with the true essence of *Chanukah*, it should come as no surprise that this holiday is fading from our cultural landscape, except perhaps for the affection continued to be felt toward jelly doughnuts and *latkes* (potato pancakes).

Although we will discuss the customs and legends associated with *Chanukah*, it seems that for us alone they do not constitute a reason for celebrating the holiday. According to one traditional belief, *Chanukah* is the holiday for childless couples. If a couple experiences infertility, it is said to be possible, by means of correct spiritual communication with *Binah* on *Rosh Hashanah* or *Chanukah*, for them to complete the missing portion of life energy—to open up the blockage, to attain a state of fertility, and to bring offspring into the world. The issue of fertility is one of the most mysterious wonders of Creation. Even today, with the replication of animals in laboratories, no one truly understands how a sperm cell and an ovum turn into a mature, living creature. Because of the enormous amount of life energy injected into our universe on *Rosh Hashanah* and *Chanukah*, if a person connects to this energy and attracts it to the world through himself, this will suffice to help him bring children into the world. It is important to note that the sages connected *Rosh Hashanah* and *Chanukah* to childless couples. I note this in order to emphasize that on *Chanukah* we do not celebrate the victory of the *Maccabim* over their enemies, but rather the cosmic event—the additional opportunity to connect to *Binah*—that comes back and is revealed at this time for all those who know how to attain the connection. This occasion also makes it possible to realize new life in the world through fertilization.

Another legend connected to the Festival of *Chanukah* is the story of Hannah and her seven sons. In *Sha'ar Hakavanot, Peri Etz Hacha'im*, or *Gate of Meditations—Fruit of the Tree of Life* (page 465), The Ari claimed that the heroine Hannah, who sacrificed herself and her seven sons for the glory of God, did so out of her aversion to the Greek culture. Her heroism stemmed not from emotional factors, however, but rather from the fact that she refused to be subjected to Greek idolatry or to the desire to receive for the self alone, preferring instead to die in the name of God. The numerical value for the name חנה (Hannah) equals 63. In addition, the combination חנה + כו forms the word חנוכה (*Chanukah*). It is therefore no accident that Hannah is center stage, as was Mattityahu. The numerical value of the Tetragrammaton (the Name of God that connects us to mercy) is 26, and therefore it expresses the power embodied in this name. But where is this force to be found, and how can we connect to it? The force is revealed during the connection of *Malchut* to *Zeir Anpin*. When Hannah traded the physical existence of the desire to receive for the self alone for a natural concept of sharing, she formed the connection with the Tetragrammaton of God.

We might also ask, What is the source of the name *Chanukah*? We know that this question is of great importance in that the biblical code is based on names. According to the meaning of the names, we can decipher the meaning of the kabbalistic holidays and festivals. Why, then, is this holiday called חנוכה (*Chanukah*)? In essence, the name is a hint—a code for understanding the meaning embodied in the holiday. When we perform the cosmic communication by means of the candle lighting blessings, the name to which we direct ourselves will be חנה, Hannah—which replies *Malchut*, or a desire to receive, the feminine aspect—and its connection with כו (26), which means *Zeir Anpin*, or a desire to share, the masculine aspect. This is the only way for us to connect to the Tetragrammaton, which in its essence portrays the vital characteristic of the desire to share. If we substitute the desire to receive for the self alone with the desire to receive for the sake of sharing, we may connect ourselves to Jupiter and Sagittarius. For that, however, additional tools, such as blessings and special meditations, are required as well. The blessings create channels and the meditations cause the electricity to flow through them, just as would occur in a physical communication network. The cables are nothing but the potential to transmit information; when the network is connected to the power supply with functioning transmitters and receivers at its ends, only then can the potential that is embodied in the hardware be realized.

The significance of the meditations is to protect us from exposure to disaster, suffering, and deprivation. This is the purpose of the cosmic opportunity of the connection called *Chanukah*. Thus, the word *Chanukah* is composed of *Malchut* + *Zeir Anpin*. This, then, is the significance of the story about Hannah and her seven sons. The seven sons represent the seven lower *Sfirot*: the six levels of *Zeir Anpin* and *Malchut* (Diagram 3). In other words, as much as the story sounds impressive and emotional, it has never caused the Israelite people to properly observe the Festival of *Chanukah* and the spiritual communication embodied within it. That is why The Ari explained it to us this way—to impress us with the spiritual communications that we will attempt to form on *Chanukah*.

And thus the holiday explains itself: The consciousness of *Malchut*, which is the desire to receive for the self alone, should be converted, and the coupling of Hannah and יהוה, the Tetragrammaton, should be formed in order to create a desire to receive for the sake of sharing. By means of this link, we connect Jupiter with Sagittarius and form a uniform entity that serves as a channel through which the energy reservoir called *Binah* causes life to flow through us through

Zeir Anpin to *Malchut* (Diagram 3). It is like the neutron, which is composed of a proton and an electron. The Tetragrammaton, the aspect of sharing, is embodied in the proton; *Malchut*, Hannah, the aspect of receiving, is embodied in the electron. When the two are connected, we obtain the key that opens the door to the energy reservoir called *Binah*.

I am not overwhelming you with information in order to impress you or convince you to observe the holiday. This is not the purpose of Kabbalah. Exposure to information is essential for two reasons: First, it allows for true freedom of choice; and second, knowledge is the connection. If a person chooses to connect on *Chanukah*, he is able to realize this connection by means of knowledge. We learn this from the interpretation presented by *The Zohar* in Exodus 4:1. "And the man knew Eve his wife; and she conceived and bore Cain . . ." *The Zohar* concludes from this verse that knowledge is the connection, the true union, and not something that is purely theoretical. The more we know, the better we can connect to the energy that Jupiter and Sagittarius conduct to the world, and connect to the meaning of the candles.

The candles we light are another important aspect we need to understand in order to grasp the meaning of *Chanukah*. What is a candle in general? And why are candles used in most methods of meditation as well as in celebrations or events with special significance? We know that a candle can provide a channel for the transfer of energy by virtue of an invisible inner structure that forms a connection between *Zeir Anpin* and *Malchut* (Diagram 3); this is evident in the two visible parts of the candle's flame, the white and the black, as well as in two additional halo-like parts that are invisible.

In essence, *Chanukah* is a "make-up round"—a last chance for stragglers to complete the connection to the life force and protection they are lacking in order to arrive at *Rosh Hashanah* the following year both healthy and whole. How, then, do we attain this communication with the Light? By lighting the candles of the *Chanukiah*. Here again, it has nothing to do with the military victory over the Greeks. The Greek empire relied on the forces of darkness, which are connected to the consciousness of illusion and to the desire to receive for the self alone. The moment Light is revealed in the world, it is necessary that darkness disappear. Therefore, the miracle of *Chanukah* caused the fall of the Greeks and the disintegration of their kingdom.

Today, in order to rouse the revelation of that same power, all we need do is light the lights. To truly achieve this objective, however, we must share similarity of form with the Light. This means that we must be in a state of sharing and caring for others; we must be the initiators and not the reactors. We must have control over our spirits and must not be slaves to our natural tendencies and weaknesses, which are dictated by the planets and constellations. But all these are only means of attaining the objective: the connection to the Light and its revelation. The Light is not diminished if it is in a state of giving and sharing, just as would be the case with the flame of a candle. If a candle lights another candle, the flame of the original light does not diminish. This does not hold true when we divide a piece of cake into two, or when water is poured from one glass to another. In general, anything transferred to the second element comes at the expense of the first. Only the flame of a candle is not subject to this law, reflecting the intrinsic quality the candle shares with the Light force of the Creator. This, then, is the connection between the *Chanukiah* candles and the cosmic event that takes place on this holiday: To connect to the Light, we must learn how to give and share from the candle's flame. And this is why the oil jar was discovered and the menorah lit: to teach us how to have similar form with the Light.

Numerology is of great value in Kabbalah. It may be said that *Gematria*—the numerology of the Aramaic alphabet—is to the kabbalist as mathematics is to the physicist. The numerical value of the Aramaic word נֵר *ner* (candle) is 250. In this case as well, the candle did not get its name by chance. Instead, the name hints at the inner essence of the object. Just as 63 is the magic number for the cosmic entities Jupiter and Sagittarius, so too is 250 the magic number for the candle-lighting meditations.

Why are the candles not all lit at once? And why does Shammai instruct us to deduct the number of candles in the *Chanukiah* each day from 8 to 1? This may be understood through use of one of the most important spiritual rules, which is called "reciprocity between the Light and the vessel." This rule explains that while spiritually the higher *Sfirot* are purer vessels—having less desire to receive and being closer to the Light—they nevertheless involve a smaller revelation of Light, like the sides of the vessel. In contrast, the bottom of the vessel, which is the lowest level—including the level of *Malchut*, which is the most base—affords a greater revelation of Light by virtue of the refraction of Light, the greatest force of resistance, for it is there that the desire to receive is greatest.

Let us now examine the controversy between Shammai and Hillel regarding the lighting of the *Chanukah* candles. We recall that Hillel said that we must begin with the lighting of a single candle and finish with a full *Chanukiah*, whereas Shammai said that we must begin with a full *Chanukiah* and finish with a single candle. Shammai described things from the point of view of the Age of Aquarius. We are advancing toward Messiah consciousness. As long as the Messiah has not yet been revealed in the world, the split is recognizable by the flames of the various candles. After the Messiah's revelation we can achieve unity, and this will be expressed by the single candle. Hillel describes things from the perspective of the realm of *Malchut*, prior to the revelation of the Messiah and that we begin lighting one candle and finish with a full Chanukiah, this is the path to be taken toward deliverance. The way to redeem the world is to reveal more and more Light until the total removal of chaos has been attained.

Throughout the holiday, the universe is injected with energy of life, and all that is left for us to do is connect to it. And to do so, we light candles. Do not get the impression, however, that the lighting of the candles is the only thing that must be done. Candles have been lit for hundreds of years, but we have yet to witness an amazing revelation of "love your neighbor as yourself" as a direct result. Nor have we seen a significant improvement in life expectancy or a resistance to natural catastrophes or other disasters.

In order for us to connect to the energy injected into the universe on *Chanukah*, two things must be known: first, why we light the candles, and second, how we light them. In what way must they be lit, and with what consciousness? In *Sha'ar Hakavanot*, or *Gate of Meditations*, The Ari describes the precise manner in which to use the power of thought while lighting the candles. Without integrating the meditations into the act of lighting, one cannot connect to the Light force that is revealed on *Chanukah*. Those who do not know the reason for lighting the candles cannot connect to the Light.

In *Sha'ar Hakavanot*, or *Gate of Meditations* (volume 2, page 326, first column), The Ari explains the sanctity of these days. During the week, *Malchut* draws its Light through *Zeir Anpin*, and Jacob draws his Light from *Netzach* and *Hod* and passes the Light on to Rachel. On *Chanukah* and *Purim*, more sanctity exists than on ordinary days, and as a result, Rachel and *Malchut* can draw their Light directly from *Hod* rather than through Jacob. This puts a temporary stop to Rachel's dependence on Jacob, which is characteristic of regular days. Incidentally, on *Shabbat*, holidays, and every *Rosh Chodesh*, there is more sanctity than on *Chanukah* and *Purim*, but these are explained each in its place. In *Pri Etz Cha'im*, or *Fruit of the Tree of Life* (Part 2, page 464, chapter 4, *Sha'ar Chanukah*), The Ari says:

> "The secret of the eight days of *Chanukah*; *Malchut* receives the light from *Sfirah Hod* itself, not through *Zeir Anpin*."

Malchut receives Light through the mediation of *Zeir Anpin* and not directly from *Binah*. This secret explains why we always need a mediating agent, like a resistor in an electric circuit. This is why it is impossible to connect directly to the raw energy in *Binah* (see Diagram 3).

The Ari continues:

> "During the weekdays Jacob is in *Sfirah Netzach* and Rachel is in *Sfirah Hod*, in the aspect of "for my glory was turned in me into corruption", then, *Sfirah Netzach* was corrected in the aspect of "And the victory of Israel will not lie", this is the reason that *Malchut* receives from him light through *Sfirah Hod* through *Netzach*."

The word תִקֵן *tiken* (corrected) or נִתְקֵן *nitaken* (was corrected) indicates that the same *Sfirah* serves as an available source of energy for us in *Malchut*.

> "But during these eight days Matityahu, the high priest, was correcting *Sfirah Hod* alone.

That is why (during *Chanukah*) she is receiving (Rachel, the *Malchut*) light from *Sfirah Hod* itself, and not by him (not through Jacob, through *Sfirah Netzach*). This is the reason that we say 'for the miracles' during the blessing of the *Modim* (giving thanks) which represent *Sfirah Hod*.

Up until the time of Mattityahu, no one knew that from the 25th of *Kislev* until the second of *Tevet*, one could connect directly to *Hod* without mediation. Mattityahu's discovery of this secret made the *Sfirah* of *Hod* available to us on these days, for knowledge equals connection. What is the practical significance of this discovery? What is the meaning of a direct connection to the power of *Hod*? During these days of *Chanukah*, it is possible to control matter using the power of thought. The miracle of *Chanukah* is the result of this connection to *Hod* (see Diagram 1).

The candle lighting meditations are the key to direct connection to the *Sfirah* of *Hod* and to the ability of making miracles happen. Just imagine a shop in which one could purchase the capacity to make miracles. How many people would line up at the door? If the shop were open only eight days a year, how many people would be willing to wait in line for the entire year just to be able to get in when the shop opened? The shop is the *Sfirah* of *Hod*, and *Chanukah* is its grand opening. This is the meaning of the holiday. The fact that a handful of Israelites defeated the Greek army has no bearing on our lives today and is not a reason for celebrating the holiday, but the connection to the *Sfirah* of *Hod* is indeed of immediate relevance to us today. The reason miracles have not occurred each *Chanukah* for the past 2,000 years is that people did not connect to *Hod*, just as they did not make use of the candle lighting meditations. Knowledge is the key to the connection to Light, and knowledge is what differentiates between the reality of *oy* and that of *ashrei*, woe and praiseworthy, which are the two possibilities for our existence in this Age of Aquarius. The difference lies in our consciousness.

The Ari continues:

> "And so in Chanukah, the intention of the lightning of the candles is that one should meditate to lower one's hand."

The *Chanukiah* should be lower in height than the lighter's hands so that the lighter lowers his hands during the candle lighting. For precisely the same reason, the *Shamash* must be higher than the other candles on the *Chanukiah*. The question of when to implement the candle lighting meditations then arises. The answer is simple: In the lighting of the Shamash, all the preliminary actions may be performed with the consciousness of holiday preparations, but the three *Yichudim* (unifications) are to be directed only after lighting the *Shamash*, while blessing and saying the word (*lehadlik*, or to light). This precision connects the physical, illusory act of lighting the *Shamash* with the spiritual, true act of attracting the Light to the world through ourselves. We will continue to read from the writings of The Ari: *A Kosher Menorah* must be raised at least three hand-breadths above ground level, but not more than ten hand-breadths.

We have learned from the *Ten Luminous Emanations* that when a stone is thrown into the water, all the energy's impact is revealed in expanding concentric circles, and yet the water remains perfectly still at the point of impact. In essence, the point of impact of our stone is the lighting of the *Chanukiah*. In order for the energy of the waves to be revealed in the realm of the three *Sfirot* of *Chanukah*, the *Chanukiah* must rise to a height greater than three hand-breadths, and the meeting point from which the energy is released must be above and beyond the realm of *Netzach*, *Hod*, and *Yesod*. Obviously, it must be within the range of the Ten *Sfirot*, and therefore the *Chanukiah* must not be lit at a height greater than ten hand-breadths.

Another reason for this is that *Keter*, the point of meeting, must be beyond the reach of the *klipot*, which are restricted to the range beneath *Tiferet*—namely, the lower triangle—and *Malchut*. Ordinarily, Satan gathers his energy at the meeting point unless it lies beyond his reach. This is the reason for the saying, "Sin waits at every opening." The opening of the house is the door; there it is determined whether or not one goes out and whether or not one comes in. That is where Satan waits, and that is why the *Mezuzah* (Scroll written in Aramaic placed on the doorpost) is located at the doorway and why the *Chanukiah* must face in that direction. In order to connect in a spiritual manner to the energetic event that is revealed in *Binah* of *Netzach*, *Hod*, and *Yesod*, but we will set the focal point, the *Chanukiah*, beyond the range of three hand-breadths so that we may attract the Light from the expanding circles rather than from the source. Satan seeks the Light of the *Chanukiah*, but the Light is actually *Keter* of *Netzach*, *Hod*, and *Yesod*. Just as water at the point of impact of the thrown stone is absolutely still, leaving the energy completely concealed; when the range of revelation lies beyond his reach, Satan is unable to attract Light for his needs.

Actually, potential Light is found in the ever-expanding circles, but in order for one to connect to them and reveal them in the world of illusion, it is necessary to go through the process of throwing a stone into a lake, just as we do in lighting a *Chanukiah*. To be sure, these seem to be heretical statements. How can the entire matter of lighting the *Chanukiah* be illusory and secondary in importance when there is a *Mishnah* (law) that clearly states that during the days of the Messiah, the Torah will cease to exist and the Festival of *Purim* alone will remain? Therefore, the approach that refers to the observance of the physical *mitzvot* as a temporary means to the goal of creating a connection between the two worlds is supported not only by *The Zohar* but by the *Talmud* as well. Very few are likely to dispute such renowned sources.

Keter is the point of impact: the meeting point with the uncomfortable. Therefore, if we overcome the barriers, apply restriction, and pass through the *Sfirah* of *Keter* without fear of the uncomfortable, we will be able to connect to the Light and continue from there, uninterrupted, to the Endless World. The first step, *Keter*, is crucially important for the perpetuation of the process, and the willingness to walk with it constitutes the willingness to cope with the uncomfortable. The physical expression of *Keter*, in our case, is the *Chanukiah*. We lower the Light to *Malchut* in order to fight the final and decisive battle against Satan. That is why it is written, ". . . when he lowers his hand to light."

And The Ari continues: "It's because the candelabra is above three handbreadths from the floor, it represents the *Sfirot Netsach*, *Hod*, and *Yesod* which are three handbreadths and under 10 handbreadths, which is not going above the head (the top)." And we continue to the head, attracting Light from *Keter* and not from an inferior source. We wish to focus on the meeting point of the stone with the water, only to subsequently attract the energy from the concentric waves that will spread out from this point. We have no interest in remaining at the meeting point, for nothing happens there. "So, if one put the candelabra in the zone of the ten handbreadths, one did the connection properly."

Such is the *Halachah*, or universal laws. I love to study *Halachah* because it is like studying the laws of physics. As long as we live in this world, we are bound by universal laws—but in order to obey them, we must first know them. This is the reason for studying the universal laws. But perhaps one might wonder why these are the laws and *Halachot*? The answer to this question can be found in Kabbalah. In the passage we just read, it is stated that for those who light the *Chanukiah* in the said manner, יוֹצֵא *yotzeh* (goes out)—that is, succeeds in fulfilling the *mitzvah*. Why did the author of the *Shulchan Aruch* (The Book of Laws), Rav Joseph Karo, use the word *yotzeh*? Why did the *Talmud* use the exact same word? What are we going out of? And where were we before we went out? The word *yotzeh* directs us toward the deviation that lies beyond the consciousness of illusion and the connection to the World of Truth, the connection to the Light. The authors of the *Talmud* knew this, and Rav Joseph Karo knew this. Those who do not know it cannot go out unless they have connected to this consciousness in each *mitzvah* that they fulfill.

The world of illusion and all the garments that conceal the Torah will disappear when we reach Messiah consciousness. All *mitzvot* are connected to the physical world of illusion, and therefore they too will disappear in the days of Messiah. But will the essence of the Torah disappear as well? Will the soul of the Torah become extinct? Absolutely not; to the contrary, only darkness will vanish. The meeting point will disappear. The black hole will disappear—the same black hole that is there when there is a short circuit, when light is drawn without balance and without force of resistance. This is why a short circuit leaves soot in its wake. And this is the force that caused humanity to repeat the same mistake for 2,000 years, despite the fact that it led only to misfortune and catastrophe. Meeting, impact, but no way out—this is black-hole consciousness. In the absence of true understanding, technical observation of the *mitzvah* does not suffice to discharge us of our obligation and does not take the observer out to the expanding circles that surround the point of impact. Therefore, it does not connect the observer to the Light and positivity that may be revealed as a result of the *mitzvah*.

But perhaps the question may be asked, "How can one be in *Keter* and also in *Netzach*, *Hod*, and *Yesod* at the same time?" The answer comes from another question: "When are footprints formed on the beach—when we walk on the beach or the day before, when we set the date for the stroll?" The day before, of course. If so, then we were there the entire time, from the very beginning. When the kabbalist holds the match to light the *Shamash*, he wants to hug the match. The match represents the moment before the *Sfirah* of *Keter*, the circles surrounding the meeting point from which all of the Light is revealed in the aftermath. It is as though the kabbalist says to the match, "I have always been with you, but now at last we meet." At the meeting point, when the match ignites the candle's wick, there is in fact no light, but that is exactly where Satan is drawn. At precisely the same moment, we leave the external circles and connect to the true Light. Similarly, we give Satan the foreskin at every *Brit Milah* (circumcision) and the first piece of the *challah* (bread) at each meal on *Shabbat*. Satan thinks he is at the center of the event, when in fact just the opposite is the case. Satan falls into the same trap and makes the same mistake every time.

> "Because of that (means because of the ten *Sfirot*) are called *mekoma* (her place), because she is taking light from all the Ten *Sfirot*. But from

above of the ten there shouldn't be any attempt to draw (because the is nothing above the Tree of Life—Ten *Sfirot*)"

It is possible to go from the world of *Asiyah* (action) to the world of *Yetzirah* (formation), and it is possible to pass from one parallel universe to another. We may be incarnated into this animal or that, but in each world and in every universe there is but one framework: that of the Ten *Sfirot*—never more, never less. We have learned from the third part of the *Ten Luminous Emanations* that it is better to be in *Malchut* of a higher world than in *Keter* of a lower world—or, as the saying goes, "Rather be a tail to lions than a head to foxes." This is the reason we are limited to the range of the Ten *Sfirot* of the Tree of Life and cannot deviate beyond it.

In the writings of The Ari, *Peri Etz Chaim* (chapter 4, page 464, *Sha'ar Hachanukah* (*The Gate of Chanukah*) "During the Shabbat she is rising up to his *Keter* (crown), and then her place is all over the ten, then she is called '*Shabbat Shlomo* candle' says: According to the universal law, when we light a *Chanukah* candle on the eve of *Shabbat*, we must light it prior to lighting the *Shabbat* candles, because after lighting the *Shabbat* candles we enter into a new framework—one that is above and beyond that of *Chanukah*.

Although the *Chanukah* candles draw Light through all Sfirot, *Shabbat* candles do not help us ascend to *Keter*. "So if one couldn't afford buying both oil for Shabbat candle and Chanukah candle—Shabbat candle comes first." Here The

Ari teaches us an additional lesson. Since the *Shabbat* candle elevates us to a higher level than *Chanukah* candles, why don't we skip the lower level of *Chanukah* and jump directly to the higher level of *Shabbat?* On certain occasions, we skip parts of the regular prayer service because the holiday elevates us beyond the parts over which we pass. But in this case the situation is different. The Ari explains:

> "Because it's good to raise him slowly slowly from the bottom to the top and from one level to the other, but if he already lit the *Shabbat* candles, which *Shabbat* is already is in the top – how can one, god forbid, can return it down to *Netsach – Hod – Yesod.*"

We have two issues here: first, the issue of lighting a *Chanukah* candle before a *Shabbat* candle, whose purpose is to elevate us gradually in *Sfirot* and connect us with all aspects of the Light that are revealed to us in the course of this process. The second issue is that *Chanukah* candles are not lit after *Shabbat* candles in order to prevent the Light of *Shabbat* from being passed over to Satan. During *Kabbalat Shabbat*, we prevent the *klipot* from holding on to the Light of *Shabbat* by reciting a portion from *The Zohar* entitled כְּגַוְנָא *Kegavnah*. By reciting *Kegavnah*, we block the *klipot* access to the Light by returning them to the ground and burying them there until the end of *Shabbat*. This appears to be an illusion, but since the world of illusion is the *klipah*'s realm of existence, they are subject to the influence of prayer and must disappear from the world until the end of *Shabbat*.

If the *Chanukah* candles are lit after *Shabbat* candles, the Light of *Shabbat* is lowered to the realm of *Netzach*, *Hod*, and *Yesod*, in which the *klipot* already have a hold—and thus they are, heaven forbid, nourished.

To sum up: The first issue, which deals with whether or not one should light *Chanukah* candles before *Shabbat* candles, is considered optional. It's a good recommendation that, if not followed, does not result in any harm to the world—only to the individual. Similarly, when a person uses drugs, only he suffers brain damage—not only as a result of the sudden rise to upper worlds, but also as a consequence of his having been exposed to all the Light embodied in those worlds without first preparing the vessel and applying the force of resistance. But the second issue, which deals with lighting a *Chanukah* candle after a *Shabbat* candle, is considered a strict prohibition; those who do not abide by it, cause great damage to the entire world, not just to themselves.

Lighting *Shabbat* candles elevates us to a realm in which Satan does not exist, above the ten hand-breadths of the *Chanukiah*. There is, however, an additional difference between *Shabbat* candles and *Chanukah* candles. A *Shabbat* candle connects us to *Shabbat*. By contrast, the *Chanukah* candle is the meeting point—the place in which the force of resistance is applied, the *Keter*, the potential without which it is not possible to reveal the Light. By lighting a *Chanukah* candle, we create a focal point from which waves expand outward, and in so doing we draw Satan to the focus where nothing actually happens while we ourselves proceed from there to the periphery and connect to the energy of the expanding circles.

From here we come to another fine universal law that has no explanation other than that of the kabbalistic discussion we are holding right now: "*Chanukah* candles are meant only to be seen, and we have no permission to make use of them." The *Chanukiah* must burn for at least half an hour. During that time we must be in the room with it, but we must not use it for light, heat, or the ignition of any other fire. If there is no other source of light in the room, we are forbidden to sit down and read a newspaper, a book, or even the Torah by the light of the candles. This prohibition does not apply to *Shabbat* candles, whose light is permitted for any use. The reason for the prohibition of the use of *Chanukah* candles is that *Netzach*, *Hod*, and *Yesod* are in the realm of Satan's existence. Any physical act and revelation of physical light performed by the light of the *Chanukiah* nourishes the *klipot* as well; unlike on *Shabbat*, in this realm Satan is in the room with us.

Here we discover beauty in the performance of spiritual work. When we practice the proper meditations, we are not performing a physical action from which Satan can benefit. When *Tefilin* (Phylacteries) are put on, nothing happens because the physical action is not the meeting place that reveals the Light. But when in the course of laying the *Tefilin* we express the intention that the *Tefilin* will bind our desire to receive for the self alone—which is essentially the purpose of performing this act—one must first recite kabbalistic meditations. The laying of non-physical *Tefilin* is the meeting point, but at this juncture it is not physical, so the *klipot* have not yet taken hold. Any person who does not recite kabbalistic meditations and does not initiate the connection of *Zeir Anpin* and *Malchut* misses out on the main part of the act, remaining entirely in the realm of the illusion, and does not attain spiritual communication with the Light. Making do with physical actions is devoid of all purpose. Every Israelite knows that man is not just dust of the earth but also the spirit within. It is evident that the spirit requires the dust in order to remove Bread of Shame. Only by forming the connection with spirituality and by means of the meditations is it possible for us to proceed from the world of illusion to the world of truth—to draw the Light and fulfill the *mitzvah*.

Before we light the candles, we first meditate on being one soul. By doing so we are able achieve the level of expertise and knowledge of a kabbalist, since this preliminary meditation unifies us all. To be sure, there are those who doubt this "mind over matter" approach. Yet no one in the world acts without thinking first, and no building is constructed without someone having first designed it. Thus, the principle of thought before action, or mind over matter, is a general one that is reflected in all areas of life, and it is one that cannot be ignored. Furthermore, since we are all made of atoms, and since the atoms that make up one man are identical to those that make up his fellow man, we have good reason to believe that such unity is indeed possible. We also know that the physical body gives us the illusion that we are different from one another. For all these reasons, the meditation of unity is important both in practice and in realization. The more people participate, the greater the effect of the unity. Like a cable made of many fibers, its strength is not just the sum of that of the fibers, but much more than that. This is why we perform the communication while we meditate on being one soul, and the person lighting the candles directs us all.

It should be understood that the issue of unity does not contradict the fact that no two human beings are identical. Each person comes into the world to discover a different aspect of the Creator and to correct a different part of Adam's soul. Each person has a specific mission in the world. But all human beings serve like cells in a single body: Although they are separate and defined, they are at the same time aware of one another, supportive of one another, and acting jointly in the realization of common goals at the tissue level, the organ level, and the corporeal level. Unity of variance is the key to salvation.

Shabbat candles are always lit at sunset. The reason for this requires an understanding of a phenomenon that occurs at sunset. An article in Time magazine once described a study in which it was revealed that most crimes are committed between 5 and 7 PM Do we think that the logical explanation for this phenomenon is that there was an international conference of thieves in which it was decided that the hours between 5 and 7 PM are the most suitable for crime? The Ari, however, offers a more profound explanation of this phenomenon—and one that existed long before the writing of the article in *Time*. In short, The Ari reveals that during these hours, cosmic activity takes place in which an increase in negativity occurs in the world. Hence we learn that it is not possible to avoid taking responsibility for everything that happens to us in life. In order to connect to the Light, it is necessary for us to overcome an aspect of darkness, take responsibility, and act proactively lest we return to the original problem of the accumulation of Bread of Shame. If all were good and easy, there would be no reason for human existence. Obviously our existence is related to the fact that each of us has a role to play—a specific, defined contribution to the general good. This concept, however, is not self-evident. A contribution to family and friends is perhaps more easily understood, but a contribution to all of mankind and the universe is more difficult to imagine.

The existence of negativity in the world is necessary so that we may overcome it, and in so doing remove Bread of Shame. This negativity is injected into the world every evening at sunset. Those who take things that do not belong to them and who fail to restrict this tendency can fall under the influence of the increased negativity that takes place every evening close to sunset. Since the lighting of the *Chanukah* candles was intended to rid the world of negativity by revealing Light, we perform this act precisely when negativity is increasing—that is to say, close to sunset. On the eve of *Shabbat*, since *Chanukah* candle lighting must precede that of the *Shabbat* candle lighting, we light the *Chanukiah* a bit earlier. We do not light *Chanukah* candles during the day, when *Zeir Anpin* rules the world, for at this time negativity cannot hold its head up high, and the candles would burn in vain.

The greatest power described in the Torah that provides the absolute cosmic connection for drawing the energies of the universe is the Tetragrammaton. Although this concept may at first seem complex, I am certain we will be able to understand the thought that underlies it if we discuss it slowly and deliberately. The Tetragrammaton is basically composed of four Aramaic letters: י (*Yud*), ה (*Hei*), ו (*Vav*), and another ה (*Hei*). The word יוד is composed of the letter י (*Yud*) and two additional letters: ו (*Vav*) and ד (*Dalet*). That numerical value of the word is 20. The second letter, when pronounced as a word, is composed of the letter ה (*Hei*) and the letter י (*Yud*). The numerical value of the word הי is 15. The third letter, when pronounced as a word, is composed of the letter ו (*Vav*) and the letters י (*Yud*) and again ו (*Vav*). The numerical value of the word ויו is 22. Therefore, the sum of the values of the four words (*Yud, Hei, Vav, Hei*) is 72. A word that describes a letter is called the "full form" (*milui*) of that letter. The letters that complete the word, not including the first letter, are called the filling. The full form is a kind of extended expression of the reduced letter. The numerical value of the reduced expression of the Tetragrammaton is 26. This name is not uttered in Aramaic, neither out loud nor even as a whisper. If we were to do so, our thoughts would have to be completely pure. Otherwise the immense power that this name when we utter it might harm us, due to the lack of purity of our vessel to the intensity of Light passing through us. After we expand the

Tetragrammaton, it is as if we have covered it with camouflage, and in this shape it may be pronounced without fear.

In The Ari's *Pri Etz Chaim* (Volume 2, page 464, second column), it is said, "And here *Chanukah* is only in *Netzach – Hod – Yesod*" *Chanukah* is found only in the framework of reference of the Magen David's lower triangle. We did not mention these things earlier, for without a basic understanding of the Ten *Sfirot*, such a statement might create frustration; inability to crack the code conflicts with the desire to receive for the self alone and only causes it to strengthen without balance. On the other hand, this revelation enables those who are familiar with *Netzach*, *Hod*, and *Yesod* to make an immediate connection to the energy of *Chanukah*—a connection that forms a cycle of energy, bringing about satisfaction and fulfillment, and balances and soothes the desire to receive for oneself. *Chanukah* is connected to the lower triangle of the Ten *Sfirot*. Beyond it is the upper triangle— *Chesed*, *Gvurah*, and *Tiferet*—and beyond that is the realm of the three first *Sfirot*: the world of all or nothing; the realm of *Keter*, *Chochmah*, and *Binah* or *Chochmah*, *Binah*, and *Da'at*. (Diagram 3)

The same holds true for the parts of the Torah that do not contain any print. According to *The Zohar*, the print is *Malchut*, the execution of information encrypted in the Torah, while the empty sections contain all the energy that is related to the higher *Sfirot*. Therefore it is said that we should "read between the lines." Occasionally, however, we forget this and concentrate only on what is written. In fact, there is Light between the lines even before we try to connect to it, just as there is light in a dark room even before we turn on the light. The Light is in an encoded, potential, and hidden state. Seeing that this is so, the realization and revelation of the potential necessitate a gradual passage through all *Sfirot* up until *Malchut*.

The Ari tells us that *Chanukah* is connected only to the *Sfirot* of *Netzach*, *Hod*, and *Yesod*. This tells us that the energy of the holiday is focused and available to us, more so than the energy of *Keter*. In *Keter* the energy is in a potential state, like the light in a dark room. When the light is turned on, light is indeed revealed, but it is also restricted in terms of its range and intensity. By contrast, when the Light is only in a potential state, it is unlimited. We even have tangible, common evidence of this: Prices in candlelit restaurants are higher than in those illuminated by neon lights. Less light means more money. Candlelight leaves more room for the imagination. This is a paradox that is studied only in the *Ten Luminous Emanations*.

Yesod and *Malchut*, which are also embodied in the last two days of *Chanukah*, are closely related to one another, and on *Chanukah* both are reinforced by the power of *Rosh Chodesh Tevet* (Capricorn) as well. During these two days, in addition to the power we receive from the lighting of the *Chanukiah*—and in addition to the connection to the Light that we performed from the beginning of the holiday (a connection that removes the chaos from our lives)—we are also granted a further level of sanctity that is uncovered on *Rosh*

Chodesh. *Rosh Chodesh* falling on the last two days of *Chanukah*, together with the letters of the month, are proof—a kind of fingerprint of the Creator—that there are no coincidences. The world was created in a wonderfully orderly and planned pattern. With all the knowledge revealed to us regarding the full meaning of *Chanukah*, we are approaching the end of the age of chaos, as Rav Abraham Azulai predicted, and are nearing the reign of mind over matter. Miracles will become the norm and chaos will be considered a miracle—a deviation from the perfect, balanced, and harmonious nature of the universe.

Every day we gradually build the Light of miracles, adding candles to the *Chanukiah*. But the miracle did not end on the eighth day of *Chanukah* in the days of the *Maccabim*; it is still here with us today. We are in the movie *Raiders of the Lost Ark*, and the day will come when we will discover the ark in its entirety. The last day of *Chanukah* is called זאת חנוכה *Zot Chanukah* (This is *Chanukah*). The day is given this name because it is time to connect—to take advantage of the opportunity to remove chaos from life, to give the mind control over matter, and to perform a miracle. We have absolutely no justification for looking up to heaven and asking the Creator to perform a miracle for us, for the Creator replied to this plea 3,400 years ago (Exodus 14:15). "Why are you crying to Me?" We have had the tools to perform miracles for thousands of years.

It is a great privilege to be alive today, when all of this knowledge is being exposed. At the same time, however, we must again ask, "Why me? Why did I have the good fortune to attain the knowledge that was concealed from generations of righteous Israelites before me? Was Rav Akiva not more important than me? Was he not more worthy of the revelation of this knowledge?" But by virtue of the spiritual work done by Rav Akiva and the righteous men who followed him, which caused the accumulation of so much positive energy in the universe, we, the lowly sons of *Malchut*, have achieved the revelation and execution of all that energy. *Malchut* executes all the potential Light that has accumulated in the preceding *Sfirot*. We must therefore appreciate the enormous privilege we were given to realize the concept of *bila hamavet lanetzach* (death will be swallowed forever) in these lives of ours. We shout ויתנשׂא *vayitnaseh* (and he will rise) during the *Kaddish* (our stepping stone to the next level during the prayers) so as not to fall into the robotic consciousness that many sink into. It is very easy to fall into a routine pattern of prayer. We must continue to inject this consciousness into the universe until the miracle happens. No one else will do it. The power of Messiah will be revealed through all of us together. Everyone who considers himself the Messiah is either hospitalized in a mental institution or on his way to one. Why do only the insane believe themselves to be Messiah? It is because they are constantly preoccupied with themselves. But the concept of the collective messianism saves us from this mistake. I am not better than you, and I am not more important than you. I need your help in order to bring salvation to the world. Just a bit more Light is needed in order to bring about the cosmic revolution, and each and every one of us is obliged to do his best to add to and reveal this Light.

Several years ago no one in the world spoke of eternal life, yet today the entire world is talking of it. Today materialism is not just an arena for the revelation of chaos but for the revelation of mind over matter and eternal life as well. In order for that to happen, our consciousness must be in the right place.

Rosh Chodesh Shvat
(AQUARIUS)

*I*n order to understand the month of *Shvat*, we must first understand the meaning and the consciousness of the constellation of Aquarius, and of the Age of Aquarius in which we are now living. Rav Isaac Luria—The Ari—stated that in his generation, 450 years ago, we had entered the final stage of attaining freedom and deliverance. Now, in this generation, we are fortunate to see the revelation of all future knowledge. This generation is called דור דעה *dor de'ah* (generation of knowledge). This means that people living today are the reincarnation of the original generation of knowledge, the generation that left Egypt. We are not a new generation; we are an old generation reborn. As King Solomon said, "There is nothing new under the sun."

Not long ago, astrophysicists informed us of the discovery of two new planets in the solar system. The scientists did not create the planets; they just identified something that was already present but had previously gone unnoticed. This is characteristic of the generation of knowledge—the Information Age in which all that has been concealed will be uncovered.

But how can we connect with the knowledge that is now hidden? How can it be made available to us so that we can use it to realize our objectives? To achieve this, we should concentrate on one objective only—an aim that includes all the possible objectives you have thought about and those you have never even imagined.

This single aim is nothing less than the end to chaos! We are so far from this concept that it is difficult to understand its meaning. Has anyone experienced life without chaos? We have all had pain, suffering, and death in our lives. Nevertheless, 3,400 years ago, at the foot of Mount Sinai, the end of chaos was at hand. Then came the Sin of the Golden Calf. We of this generation are the very ones who brought chaos back into the universe. We are the same group of people whose objectives and aspirations remained in the consciousness of the desire to receive for the self alone.

At the time of the Sin of the Golden Calf, only the women rebelled and refused to participate or support in its creation. Those righteous women have come back in our generation with an obligation to continue the battle against chaos—a battle they began 3,400 years ago. They are the ones who are leading the revolution for the reinstatement of a sane way of life throughout the entire world.

For kabbalists, the Age of Aquarius has but one meaning: the removal of chaos from the universe. Simply put, this is a state called Messiah, or Messiah. On this issue, different religions express a variety of opinions. There are those who claim that the Messiah revealed himself 2,000 years ago. Others claim that he has yet to come but is destined to be appear shortly. Some people expect the Messiah to descend on them from heaven, while others are not even that pleased at his pending arrival. How will things be after the coming of the Messiah? Change is indeed expected, but it is not clear to most of us what lies in store. The Ari, however, was very clear that nothing will change, except that chaos will disappear from the world.

Who is the Messiah? The Ari explains that the Messiah is "he who led the Israelites out of Egypt against their will." Had the Israelites truly been unhappy in Egypt—had they truly been held there against their will, like prisoners in a cell—they would not have been so quick to ask Moses to take them back to Egypt. This is very peculiar, for every year at *Pesach* we celebrate the exodus from slavery to freedom. Yet if the Israelites were not slaves as we understand that term today, then what kind slavery is alluded to at *Pesach*? What kind of freedom did they experience? Did the people of Israel not wish for freedom? And why was it necessary to labor so hard in order to bring the Israelites out from Egypt? The Torah tells us: When Moses turned to the Israelites and said that the Creator was prepared to take them out of Egypt, they replied: We have no time for this.

It is not necessary to be in jail in order to be a prisoner. Chaos is the real prison. According to The Ari, the word freedom has only one meaning: freedom from chaos, or *bila hamavet lanetzach*. For thousands of years, negative consciousness has caused society to believe that the Festival of Freedom is about emigration, the exodus of the Israelites from Egypt. This consciousness has prevented people from discovering the true meaning of the night of the *Seder* and of the Feast of *Pesach*.

A story is told by the Ba'al Shem Tov (world renowned 18th century Kabbalist) about a king who contracted an illness that no one knew how to cure. The king offered a reward to anyone who could cure him. Whoever succeeded in doing so, said the king, would be given access to the royal treasury room for two hours, during which time he would be permitted to gather as many treasures as he could—and those treasures would be his to keep. One day a person arrived who succeeded in curing the king. Yet even though the king was obligated to honor his word, he nonetheless sought to avoid having to do so. Then one of the king's advisers told him that the man who had cured him was an avid music lover, and that whenever he heard his favorite music, he would forget where he was and would sit down and listen to the magical notes, oblivious to his surroundings. So on the designated day, the king brought a symphony to the safe room, and when the man arrived to collect his prize, the orchestra began to play his favorite pieces. The man forgot about the prize and sat down to listen with overt pleasure. Two hours later the music ended, and the man did not have the opportunity to enter the safe for even a single second. Had he entered the safe despite the music, he could later have engaged the orchestra's services and listened to music in his own home for the rest of his life.

In a similar manner, when the possibility existed to leave Egypt, the Israelites were busy with their current affairs, just as we are today. At times we are so preoccupied that we do not stop even for a moment to ask ourselves whether our current endeavors can prevent chaos in our lives. If they cannot do so, it might be better for us to perform actions that will ensure our well-being and health, and only then find the time for our various occupations. Can any of us look in the mirror and state that we have dedicated a substantial portion of our time and effort to the removal of chaos? No one can, and for two reasons: First, we have always been taught that chaos is an inevitable part of our lives. Second, we ignore this knowledge and permit Satan consciousness to anesthetize us and lead us astray. Indeed, for 2,000 years, comfortable and pleasant times have been replaced by significantly more unpleasant times, but we "know" that this time will be different. As with any other of Satan's tricks, this illusion has no factual basis. Why not dedicate a bit of our time to something truly important? Why do we choose to become addicted to music? The Ari answers this question: We act in this manner because we are not connected to the consciousness of true freedom.

If the world's peoples were asked to describe their greatest aspirations, very few would answer "to be free of chaos." Chaos manifests itself in all areas of life, but when we encounter a problem, few among us attempt to address it at its source. Everyone seeks a way to circumvent the immediate problem, but no one tries to end chaos. A temporary, superficial, symptomatic solution—this is all that is offered to us by physicians, scientists, and politicians. This has been the practice for many generations, and it is why we are unfamiliar with true freedom.

The Opponent has positioned us within a frame of consciousness that from his vantage point is perfect. We are "too busy" to consider how to override chaos. As simple as it may sound, if each and every one of us honestly examined his or her personal awareness, we would discover that we are not involved in any activity that is aimed at removing chaos from our lives. The Israelites were in a similar situation. When Moses came to them and wished to take them out of Egypt, his intention was not merely immigration, for leaving a physical jail does not constitute a guarantee against reentering that jail or another. We encounter in life a large variety of prisons that are tailor-made for each and every person.

The concept of the Messiah and an understanding of that concept can connect us to the meaning of this month, as well as to its power for ending chaos. When Abraham the Patriarch used the constellation of Aquarius to indicate the month of *Shvat*, did he thereupon determine the Israelites' release from Egyptian exile? The Israelites left Egypt in the month of *Nissan*. In addition, the *Talmud* tells us that Final Redemption will also occur during the month of *Nissan*. If so, what is the meaning of the connection between Aquarius, the constellation of redemption and the Messiah, and the month of *Shvat*?

Let us pose yet another question: When is the Messiah destined to be born? Many have already lost hope and no longer await his arrival. Others wait with bated breath. Still others have abandoned the idea of the Messiah and their belief in him. Most people are preoccupied with their daily troubles and are not free to be delivered, as was the case 3,400 years ago. Furthermore, Kabbalah tells us that the actual concept of waiting for a person to come and redeem us is faulty as well as futile.

Abraham revealed in *The Book of Formation* that the Creator had injected the universe with thought consciousness in the form of the month of *Shvat*, the constellation of Aquarius. We await the Messiah, but even if he shows up—as Moses did in his time—we will probably be too preoccupied to find time for him. The Ari tells us that Moses reveals himself in every generation. He wishes to remove chaos from all of our lives—from all of mankind and from the entire world. He attempts to help us, but we pay no attention to him.

But now the revolution can no longer be stopped. Today, millions of people are being exposed to the knowledge of Kabbalah as never before. Thus, it is no longer possible to revert and lock this knowledge up. Even Rav Shimon assures us of this (*Zohar*, Volume 13, Portion *Naso*, Section 103). The Ari warned us that the moment the news is out and reaches the ears of the *Erev Rav*—the mixed multitude—they will do everything in their power to prevent the dissemination of Kabbalah to the public. But they will not succeed, for masses of people are now involved in this process. Millions of people are already studying Kabbalah in one form or another.

The Ari explains that when we study the birth of the Messiah on *Tisha B'Av* (the ninth of *Av*), the issue lies in the consciousness of the constellation of Leo, the numerical value of which is 216—exactly the number of letters in the 72 Names of God. The 72 Names of God are the key and answer to all of mankind's ills. It is the Messiah we have been awaiting. But the Messiah is here already. The Messiah has arrived!

Knowledge of the 72 Names of God was concealed for 2,000 years. Until several years ago, only a handful of people knew that the 72 Names of God is the Messiah. Rav Shimon tells us that by using this knowledge, chaos may be removed from the entire universe. Moses, who parted the Red Sea using the 72 Names of God, is trying to communicate this to us. He is here, but we are impatient and do not have the time to listen to him, because negativity has anesthetized us for 2,000 years.

What is the power to which we can connect during the month of *Shvat*? For years I wondered how to get through the week without drawing the necessary power by reading the Torah on *Shabbat*. Even with this conduit of energy, however, we still fight chaos during the week. But without the reading of the Torah on *Shabbat*, we have no chance to rid our lives of chaos. Yet when we try to invite friends to synagogue on *Shabbat* morning, we typically hear responses such as "I am sleeping," "I have to take my kid to a soccer game," or "I don't have time." Although it is true that we have little time at our disposal, how is it that no one gives any thought to the time we waste as a result of the presence of chaos in our lives? Even a short reading of the Torah can save us many hours of troubleshooting and repairs during the week.

Why do we give in to the pathetic excuses that leave the Opponent on his throne in our lives? Without reading the Torah on *Shabbat* with the correct consciousness, no one has any chance of removing chaos from his life. Two thousand years of history proves this. In *The Book of Formation*, Abraham revealed that once a year we have an opportunity to connect to the consciousness that will bring us to a state of deliverance. This consciousness tells us not to stop looking, even for a moment, for the key to a chaos-free life. But until we spend every day and every moment thinking about being free of chaos, we will not succeed in freeing ourselves. Scientists also agree that there is nothing in the world except consciousness and its manifestations. Only by achieving the correct consciousness is it possible to ensure the required result of a chaos-free world. Without this consciousness, you will not achieve freedom even if you come to synagogue on *Shabbat* and listen regularly to the reading from the Torah. Only by focusing one's consciousness on the objective is it possible for us to attain and realize deliverance from chaos for the entire world.

But where will we draw the power to maintain this consciousness, as impatient as we are about our current affairs? Where will we find the time to contemplate redemption, the Messiah, and freedom from chaos? This is the role of the month of *Shvat*. During this month we receive the strength we need in order to maintain this consciousness every day of the year, so that we do not forget even for a moment our commitment and responsibility for freeing the entire universe from of chaos, both now and forever.

Tu Bishvat
(15TH OF AQUARIUS)

Tu Bishvat is known as the New Year of the Trees. What are we to make of this strange holiday? On *Rosh Hashanah* we observe the New Year, and all human beings are judged. But what exactly takes place on the New Year of the Trees? Do the trees and flowers stand trial before the throne of honor? And what did they do or not do in the course of the year that is worthy of passing judgment? On this day, traditionalists eat delicacies made of fruit or plant new trees—the holiday's primary purpose in the eyes of people around the world who have not studied Kabbalah. There are no prayers, no meditations, no repentance, and no special demands made on us. Even if you do not eat any fruit, you have not sinned. This day can pass without leaving any impression on your life. Why, then, is there any need to take note of this day?

Tu Bishvat is the day on which all members of the vegetable kingdom receive their annual portion of energy. The New Year of the Trees means that on this day, plants are born and receive a new portion of life, just as human beings do in the month of *Tishrei*. The world exists on annual portions of energy given to it every *Rosh Hashanah*. For the same reason sound emanates from a radio for a moment after it has been switched off, we do not see all human beings fall to the ground and die in the split second that passes between the time we finish the life energy from the previous year and the time we receive the new portion of energy. Still, this is what happens on a spiritual level. And from a spiritual point of view, all trees die and are renewed on *Tu Bishvat*. A tree that does not receive the portion of life for the new year will wither and die in the course of the year. If it is a fruit-bearing variety, it will not bear fruit.

In the matter of *Tu Bishvat*, *The Zohar* refers us to the *Talmud*. The appropriate chapter in the *Talmud* specifies four New Year celebrations. From our knowledge of Kabbalah, we immediately understand that the number four is connected with *Chochmah*, *Binah*, *Zeir Anpin*, and *Malchut*, the four levels embodied in the *Tetragrammaton*—just like the four fingers and the thumb, the four colors in the human eye, and the four kingdoms of nature (the human kingdom, the animal kingdom, the vegetable kingdom, and the inanimate kingdom). Each kingdom and each level of consciousness has its own *Rosh Hashanah*. Naturally, without Kabbalah, the logic underlying the existence of more than one *Rosh Hashanah* cannot be understood.

The holiday of *Pesach* takes place on the 15th of *Nissan*, when all varieties of grain and wheat are judged. Animals are judged on *Rosh Chodesh Elul*. Human beings are judged on *Rosh Chodesh Tishrei*, and the various kinds of plants are judged on *Tu Bishvat*. Incidentally, it is now commonly known that the term "inanimate kingdom" is outdated and inaccurate. Rocks or tables, which appear lifeless, are in fact made up of atoms that are in constant motion. Furthermore, subatomic behavior—which is characterized at times as particle-like and at times as wavelike—as well as the structure of the atom, which is mostly a space devoid of physical content, point to the fact that atoms are no more than a vibrating life expression of thought consciousness. When we count years, we are not specifying only their ordinal number from the moment of Creation; we are determining the frequency of resonance that enhances and organizes energy, thought consciousness, and all atoms in the world. Similarly, when Betzalel built the Ark in the Tabernacle, he did so according to exact measurements. The numerical value of those measurements was intended to determine the way in which the Ark would function and reveal Light in the physical world. Therefore, just as nobody refers to an engineer as a mystic, so too should *Gematria* (kabbalistic numerology) not be regarded as a mystical system. *Gematria* is the quantitative basis on which the entire world operates. Four New Years are connected to the four aforementioned kingdoms as well as to the four elements—fire, water, air, and earth—that represent four energetic qualities, four degrees of internal consciousness.

Many people greet each other on the first of *Tishrei* with the greeting *Shanah Tovah* (Happy New Year), as if the difference between Judaism and Christianity lies solely in the date on which the New Year is celebrated. This is one of the most common mistakes made by those who have not yet studied Kabbalah. The Torah itself states that the month of *Tishrei* is the seventh month. If this is so, however, how can it be the beginning of the new year, like January 1 on the Gregorian calendar? And if we were to greet each other with *Shanah Tovah* on the first of *Nissan*, would the mistake thus be corrected? Does the first day of the year have only chronological meaning, as if the calendar had been determined many years ago by some random person?

The true meaning of *Rosh Hashanah* cannot possibly be connected to the beginning of the year. In the kabbalistic calendar, *Rosh Hashanah* is connected to the internal energy revealed on these days throughout the entire universe. This day conceals the seed, the *Keter*, the potential of everything that is destined to take place over the course of the year. Although the seed is small and the tree is large, anyone who has studied Kabbalah knows the paradox of more is less and less is more. This means that there is more power in the seed than there is in the entire tree, but the power of the seed is potential while that of the tree is manifested. This principle is also expressed in the atom, which, despite being the smallest building block of the universe, is also the most concentrated and powerful source of energy. So too does the seed contain all future growth and potential of the tree: all branches, leaves, and fruit, and all the trees that will grow from the seeds of that fruit. On the other hand, the more revelation, the less potential: The trunk of the tree contains everything except the roots, the branch does not contain the trunk and all other branches, the leaf does not contain the branch, and so on.

The four New Years are four different manifestations of the Light of the Creator. We have mentioned that there are four kingdoms in the universe. Plants are the link between the inanimate and the animate. Each of the four New Years expresses the idea that each year we are sustained by a portion of energy that lasts for one year only. This portion is divided into four kinds of thought consciousness. We receive one of the four levels on each New Year, at which time one of the four aspects from which the world is composed is renewed.

Each New Year represents the idea that at this moment—on this day of the year—energy is replenished in one of the four kingdoms, whether inanimate, vegetable, animate, or human. The process of erosion may be seen as an example of death in the kingdom of the inanimate—mountains erode and shorelines recede. If the cause were only torrential waters, then all shorelines and mountains would be eroded to the same degree. The fact that this is not the case reveals the truth: The fate of a certain shoreline is determined by the portion of energy it received that year, and the sea waves only execute the verdict. If the shore were granted life, then sand brought in by the waves would be deposited on the shore, and the shoreline would grow. If it were doomed to extinction, the waves would erode the shoreline and gradually destroy it. All of the various creatures exhaust their allocated life energy, just as a flashlight exhausts the battery that sustains it. The minute the battery is exhausted, the flashlight goes out. This applies to all creatures in all four kingdoms. We do not see people drop dead in the streets during *Tishrei* and then come back to life, but that is not sufficient evidence to testify to the falsity of the claim.

Why are the trees and plants judged on *Tu Bishvat*, under the constellation of Aquarius? As it is known, the Israelites were freed from their exile in Egypt and began their journey toward the Promised Land during *Nissan*. The *Talmud* and *The Zohar* say that the next time redemption takes place—and this time it will be for all mankind—it will be in *Nissan* once again.

The month of *Shvat* is connected to the constellation of Aquarius. The connection was formed by Abraham the Patriarch and was first documented in *The Book of Formation*. The month's consciousness is related to the Messiah. The constellation of Aquarius depicts a woman pouring water from a jug or a pail. The ruling planet is Saturn. These are the basic facts pertaining to this month.

Why did Abraham mark the month of *Shvat*, the constellation of Aquarius, as a framework in which Messiah consciousness would be revealed throughout the world? The answer is that the Messiah that will deliver the world from chaos will indeed be revealed in *Nissan*. But Abraham determined that the month of *Shvat* would be the month of the Messiah, because during that month everyone who knows the secret is given an opportunity to connect to and reveal a personal Messiah even if the entire world is still in a state of chaos. In other words, if we have the ability to attract the energy of the month of *Shvat* in the form of a perfect connection, then we enjoy life in a new reality—one that is completely free from the chaos of the Tree of Knowledge of Good and Evil.

Let us now return to the question of the date. Why is the New Year of the Trees celebrated on the 15th day of *Shvat*? Consider this: kabbalistically, Tuesday is considered a positive day. Every student of Kabbalah knows that Tuesday is not a framework of time but rather one of thought consciousness. On this day every week, the energy of the central column and the force of balance, harmony, life, and peace are revealed in the world. On Tuesday of every week, we can connect to the force that removes chaos from life. A similar connection is also possible on the eve of *Rosh Chodesh* and on the 15th of every month. This is why these are the two times each month that the righteous come to our assistance. The righteous represent *Zeir Anpin*, above and beyond illusion and chaos. Illusion and chaos cannot reach us except on days when *Malchut* achieves complete connection with *Zeir Anpin*, on the New Moon and on the 15th day of the month. The moon is full on the 15th day of the Lunar month. Therefore, there is a full revelation of cosmic energy on that day.

A controversy exists between the great sages Hillel and Shammai as to the date of the New Year of the Trees. Shammai claims that it falls on *Rosh Chodesh Shvat*, whereas Hillel is of the opinion that it occurs on the 15th day of *Shvat*. What is the difference between these two approaches? According to *The Zohar* and the *Talmud*, both approaches are correct. The *Talmud* states, "These and these are the words of the living God." Shammai described the reality that will come to be known after the Messiah, while Hillel described reality from our viewpoint on the way to redemption, before the final revelation of the Messiah consciousness. After the Messiah comes, it will be possible to connect to the total potential embodied in the seed, as if it were already revealed. Similarly, it will be possible to draw the energy of *Tu Bishvat* as early as *Rosh Chodesh*, for this date contains the potential for all events to occur in the course of the month.

As long as the Messiah has not yet been revealed in the world, it is necessary to connect the potential with *Malchut* as a prerequisite to its revelation. This is why the sperm cell needs the egg, why a seed must be planted in the ground before it sprouts, and why we must wait until *Tu Bishvat*, when the moon appears full from the earth's vantage point. This is how we connect to the Light projected to the moon from the direction of *Zeir Anpin*. After the Messiah comes, all human beings will share a common consciousness. Until then, however, people will maintain their individual and fragmented identities, save for those whose only desire lies in the attainment of a unified human consciousness. As long as the common Messiah has not been revealed, there exists in the world an effect of fragmentation and separation—and this situation will remain until the general Messiah is revealed and the consciousness of unity reigns. Therefore, for the time being, we observe the universal law according to Hillel. On *Rosh Chodesh Shvat*, the connection between *Zeir Anpin* and *Malchut* is only in potential form. The full physical expression is attained on *Tu Bishvat*. Although Shammai claims that the New Year of the Trees falls on the first day of *Shvat* whereas Hillel contends that it falls on the 15th day of *Shvat*, both agree on the actual existence of this special energy in the month of *Shvat*, the constellation of Aquarius.

Hillel and Shammai did not quarrel with one another. They understood and knew, according to *The Zohar*, that both of their views were the words of the living God. The controversy centered only on the way in which to connect to the Light of the Creator and reveal it in the world: Should we act according to the state of the world before the revelation of the Messiah, or according to the state of the world after the revelation of the Messiah? This is also the nature of the controversy regarding the date on which the New Year of the Trees should be celebrated. *Rosh Chodesh* is and always will be the most powerful day of the month, but from the illusory point of view of the mundane world, it is on this day that *Malchut*, the moon, is dark. On the 15th day of the month, the moon appears to the earthly observer to be full. Since in the Messianic age the earthly point of view will disappear, it is written that *Sukkot* and *Pesach*—which as you know are celebrated on the 15th day of the month—will disappear as well. Until then, according to Hillel, we must refer to the illusion and celebrate the New Year of the Trees on *Tu Bishvat*, the 15th day of *Shvat*. Shammai does not disagree with that. After the Messiah is revealed, we will celebrate the holiday on the first day of *Shvat*.

In a manner similar to that of modern physical theories, *The Zohar* explains that while both Shammai and Hillel are right, each is right from his own point of view. On the 15th day, the moon is full. If we ask an astronomer about the significance of the appearance of the moon, he will tell us that appearances stem from the location of the observer in relation to the object observed. When we look at the moon from the direction of the sun, we see the side that is lit in its entirety. An astronaut on his way to the moon can see the moon in its entirety every day of the month, regardless of the way in which it is seen from earth, as long as he is looking from the sun's point of view, opposite the bright side. Shammai describes reality from the point of view of the Light, and Hillel describes reality from the point of view of the vessel. On the first day of *Shvat*, the moon appears to be dark from the side of earth, while from the direction of the sun it shines in its entirety, just as it appears to us on the 15th day of the month. Who would have imagined that a full moon appears more than once a month? Only those who connect to the spiritual information superhighway, which contains all the answers; only those who attain the same level as Shammai and Hillel can begin to grasp this concept. Incidentally, today we are deeply impressed by the Internet, which connects us to extensive information databases throughout the world. But this connection is also a source of problems—for in the absence of tools with which to analyze, organize, present, and appreciate it, this surplus of information may paralyze us by hindering our ability to choose between options and make informed decisions. In a short time we will all be connected, like Shammai and Hillel, to the spiritual Internet, compared to which today's Internet is utterly powerless.

On *Tu Bishvat* we feast on fruit not because of tradition, but because by eating the fruit we establish a physical connection with the tree consciousness that is being revealed in the universe. To be sure, eating fruit alone is not sufficient for us to form the connection to the metaphysical forces. But in the presence of the knowledge, which also is metaphysical, it is possible to make the change and connect to the power that enables the revelation of the Messiah in our lives and the perpetuation of certainty and unity throughout the entire year. The fruit represents a growth process and development from *Keter* to *Malchut* in the presence of restriction. The seed sprouts in the ground, grows constantly upward, and only then bears fruit. A man is born, applies restriction throughout his life, becomes righteous, and connects to the souls of the righteous that hold onto the Tree of Life. We do not control life, but rather the power of the Light that is found in the realm of the Tree of Life. When we are connected to this power, it guides us in a subconscious way through the paths of life and ensures our success, health, and longevity. Only the Tree of Life gives us control over our fate. On *Tu Bishvat* we can connect to Tree of Life consciousness, divert ourselves from the Tree of Knowledge of Good and Evil, and achieve Messiah consciousness on an individual level.

How is the tree related to this month? We mentioned earlier that the New Year celebrations are connected to the letters of the Tetragrammaton. Among the four aspects of the Tetragrammaton, the tree is connected to *Zeir Anpin*. It expresses the renewal of sharing consciousness and is most suitable for connection during the month of *Shvat*, for the constellation of Aquarius also represents an aspect of birth as well as a renewal of the concept of giving and caring for others. This is why in the Age of Aquarius, primarily in the last generation, so many movements have appeared that preach love, caring for others, and concern for the environment. This is the essence of the Messiah, whose appearance depends on this becoming the dominant consciousness in the world, and on defeating the desire to receive for the self alone. The reign of the desire to share over the desire to receive is represented by the essence of the tree. Long before a tree dies, it produces the next generation. Therefore, in contrast to humans, animals, and inanimate objects, the tree represents eternal continuity and, as such, connects us to the power of continuity, everlastingness, and blessing—all elements that run contrary to chaos.

On *Tu Bishvat* the tree receives the portion of energy that revives it and the power that strengthens its consciousness of sharing, enabling it to overcome the desire to receive for the self alone. By connecting to this cosmic transmission of energy, we connect ourselves to Messiah consciousness and continue to discover its effects in our lives for the next 12 months. We are not simply specifying another Talmudic or biblical detail, but rather we connect in a spiritual manner to the power that is revealed in the universe. The maintenance of this connection is the sole objective and purpose for the sake of which the Torah, our cosmic blueprint, specifies these windows in time. Any attempt to connect to the cosmic transmissions of energy through robotic observation of precepts and customs, without understanding or consciousness, is doomed to fail. According to The Ari, any precept or custom observed without understanding and consciousness of its internal essence is not observed or fulfilled at all. Without the meditations, it is not possible to be discharged of obligation.

All those who celebrate *Tu Bishvat* with the correct consciousness charge their batteries with the energy of the Messiah for an entire year. Without this spiritual charging, we can expect to be subjected to the desire to receive for the self alone, to reactivity and chaos. How do we charge the batteries? By means of the feast; by eating new fruit. This is the sole requirement. Eating the new fruit expresses the realization of the potential embodied in the tree. The fruit is the *Malchut* of the tree. Realization of the power concealed in the tree is accomplished by eating its fruit and reciting the blessing over the fruit of the tree. By eating the tree's fruit on *Tu Bishvat*, we cause the realization of all the power revealed in the universe today and permeate our lives with it. During the feast, we must meditate on attracting and sharing this consciousness with the entire world, not just with ourselves.

Rosh Chodesh Adar
(PISCES)

The month of *Adar* is governed by the astrological sign of Pisces. As *The Zohar* teaches us, *Adar* is important because it includes *Purim*, the wonderful, joyous holiday that is truly eternal. All holidays except *Purim*—including *Rosh Hashanah*, *Yom Kippur*, *Sukkot*, *Pesach*, and *Shavuot*—exist on a temporary basis, destined to disappear at the time of the Final Redemption. We may have assumed that *Yom Kippur* is the holiest day of the year, yet it is really the second most important, after *Purim*. The spiritual elevation that is achieved on *Yom Kippur* is only a humble imitation of what takes place at *Purim*. *Purim* is a cosmic event that brings our consciousness to a state of pure happiness—and through us, to the consciousness of the entire world.

According to Kabbalah, a month isn't important because a certain event might have taken place during that period. It's really quite the opposite: The event took place at a specific point because the energy revealed at the time matched that of the event and caused it to happen. This is certainly the case with regard to *Adar* and *Purim*.

What is the importance of *Purim*? From *The Book of Formation*, revealed to Abraham the Patriarch, we learn that *Chanukah* (which occurs in the month of *Kislev*, corresponding to the astrological sign of Sagittarius) and *Purim* (which occurs in the month of *Adar*, under the sign of Pisces) are both ruled by the planet Jupiter. The energy of Jupiter connects it to the consciousness of miracles. When Jupiter was designated to rule these months, it was established that Jupiter would become a channel through which the miracles of *Chanukah* and *Purim* would be revealed.

A miracle is an event of a supernatural nature. It's something we aspire to and pray for at times of crisis. *The Book of Formation* tells us that Jupiter was created for the very clear purpose of helping and supporting humankind—yet for thousands of years, this purpose was concealed. It was only in the 20th century that Rav Ashlag, the founder of The Kabbalah Centre in 1922, provided the necessary understanding of this when he made the spiritual tools of Kabbalah available to all who have a desire to learn.

Through Rav Ashlag's work, we learn that the universe exists for only one reason: to help us in the time of need. In the month of *Adar*, as in the month of *Kislev*, the miracles of *Chanukah* and *Purim* occurred as a result of the influence of

Jupiter on these two months. Both the *Maccabim* and Mordechai knew how to connect to this unique energy—how to draw it to earth and how to use it. By harnessing this knowledge, they were able to manifest miracles by breaking through limitations of time, space, and motion.

But why did the sages differentiate between *Adar* and *Kislev*? Why is it said only of *Adar* that "once this month enters, happiness prevails"? What is the difference between *Adar* and *Kislev*? And why will only *Purim* remain after the Messiah arrives?

Chanukah occurs during the astrological sign of Sagittarius, which is ruled by the letters *Samech* ס and *Gimel* ג. *Gimel* is connected to both *Adar* and *Kislev* because it created the planet Jupiter. *Kuf* ק created the sign of Pisces, and *Samech* ס created the sign of Sagittarius. This is the only obvious difference between the two months. By studying the power of the Aramaic letters from *The Zohar*, we know that the combination of *Samech* and *Gimel* is connected to the emanation of *Binah*. *Binah* is revealed on *Yom Kippur*—again, not because *Yom Kippur* is a holy day but, on the contrary, because the holiness of the day results from the revelation of *Binah*.

The revelation of the Light of *Binah* forces out all uncertainty, just as turning on a light in a room forces darkness to disappear. Light and darkness cannot coexist; this is a universal law. For humankind, darkness represents chaos. A person walking in the dark is in danger. Once light appears, however, that person can walk in safety.

Our lives exist on two parallel levels of reality: physical and spiritual. The spiritual reality cannot be grasped by the five senses, but it is real and causes results in the physical world. Without connecting to the spiritual intelligence, we are "walking in the dark " with no understanding of the events in our lives. Once we connect and "turn on the light," however, everything is revealed to us. The 20th century was full of revelations of this nature, more so than any other period in history. Why was this the case? Because of the tremendous Light revealed in the world by Rav Ashlag by opening the first Kabbalah Centre.

Where does the darkness depart when a light is turned on? And whence does it return when the light is turned off? This might seem like a childish question, but the kabbalistic answer is extremely important. *The Zohar* tells us that darkness is not only the absence of light, as physicists claim. Darkness is a physical expression of the negative side, which is responsible for all expressions of chaos in the world, including death. It is true that sporadically we can reveal Light and postpone chaos, but in the end, sooner or later, chaos reappears and death occurs. That is why, to this day, we have not met any immortals. Even if we reveal Light in the physical dimension, negative energy escapes to a different dimension. Yet it doesn't cease to exist.

But when *Adar* arrives, the influence of the letter *Kuf* ק —the only letter that extends under the line—is revealed. With regard to this issue, *The Zohar* explains that the letter *Kuf* dwells in both worlds: positive and negative, life and death. Without any nourishment, the Opponent would have perished long ago, but the letter *Kuf* nourishes him with the spiritual energy that is necessary for his existence, transferring energy from the world of life and order to that of death and chaos. On *Chanukah*, a battle was fought between the Greeks and the *Maccabim*, resulting in the victory of the *Maccabim*. But on *Purim* there was and is no battle, no army activity, that led to the fall of Haman.

Physical force was necessary on *Chanukah*, but not on *Purim*. For this reason, *Purim* is a "free" holiday, one without any restrictions. Therefore, it should be easy to celebrate this holiday. But except for parades and children's costume parties, most people make little effort to connect with the energy of *Purim*. In fact, this is a trick that the negative side plays to distract us from the real content of the holiday, which is the essence of immortality.

The fact is that *Purim* is more important than all the other holidays combined. For 2,000 years, people have been reading in *The Zohar* and the *Talmud* that *Yom Kippur* is secondary in importance to *Purim*, yet no one bothers to understand the treasure buried in this holiday. When a person fasts and prays, it does nothing to remove the negative influence from his life. It is only a form of repentance and a plea for forgiveness of our past actions, but it promises nothing for the future. *Yom Kippur* prolongs our lease in this world for another year, but it cannot promise us a happy year. Instead, we might face another year in jail or a year marked by sickness, suffering, and chaos. *Purim*, therefore, is a completely unique event.

The month of *Adar* enables us to connect to an awesome and special energy that helps us create miracles. Whoever needs a miracle in their lives had better connect to the right energy for the need. Miracles are revealed in our world through different energies, each of which correlates to the manifestation of different tasks. At the brink of the Red Sea, the Creator told Moses, "Why do you call for me? Talk to the Israelites and go forward."

The message was this: You have all the information you need. You received the 72 Names of God. Use them in the right way—connect with them to the right energies—and create any miracle you need in your lives. By using the right connection, you can turn yourselves into pipelines through which the Light of the Creator can flow, be revealed, and create the necessary changes. Therefore, you must focus your attention in yourselves by opening the channels and connecting to the right energies that will flow through you to the world. Never forget these words (Book of Exodus, portion of *Beshalach*, part 14, verse 15): *"Why do you call for me?"*

During the past 3,400 years, we have forgotten the fact that we hold the key to controlling the physical world. But it is time to remember and to take back the key. If we look back at our lives, we will discover that we have never been in control of the most important events we have witnessed, and we have never determined which way to turn at the most important crossroads, even if our ego will absolutely deny that this is the case. But the ego is merely the Opponent's servant—one that is designed to make us fail and to distract our consciousness from the truth. As long as we hold on to the idea that we are in control, we will never gain mastery over our lives.

In the month of *Adar*, we are given a unique opportunity to change this situation by using the energy of the letter *Kuf* to completely destroy the negative side forever. The Opponent, for his part, will use our ego to whisper in our ears, "Don't believe it! You cannot remove chaos with only a letter of the alphabet. Be rational; persevere in the pain and suffering that have become so familiar to you."

But the letter *Kuf* is not an ordinary letter. It is an Aramaic letter, and one that is made up of consciousness derived from a special energy that also created the astrological sign of Pisces. Every physicist will tell you that matter does not consist only of inanimate objects, but is instead made up of objects that are full of energy—objects that express themselves through endless changes and dizzying vibrations.

Perhaps no one believes that a letter can create planets, but everyone knows that DNA can create living things and determine their characteristics. Planets are significantly larger than the letter that created them—but in much the same way, a human body is much bigger than the DNA that led to its creation.

Therefore, less is more and more is less. All of our lives we have been programmed by negativity to limit our thoughts to the physical dimension. But the solution to chaos does not reside in the physical world; it lies in the manifestation of the kabbalistic knowledge with which to control the spiritual world—the true world, and that from which everything in the physical world is derived. The Aramaic letters are the keys to accomplishing this. Aramaic is the language of the universe, the language that was used to write the code by which the entire universe was created. The letter *Kuf* conceals within it the intelligent thought energy that created the sign of Pisces.

The Light of the Creator is not measured in physical terms. A small letter such as *Kuf* can contain within it the information and the intelligent energy according to which a huge constellation of stars, such as the astrological sign of Pisces, was created. This is the secret power of *Purim*. During the month of *Adar*, a force is revealed that makes truly miraculous events possible. This is more important today than ever before. We are approaching technological breakthroughs that will manifest immortality and other huge transformations that we can't even imagine. All this is possible only because of the Light revealed by the study of Kabbalah in the world as a whole. Let us remember this during the month of *Adar*, and let us make the most of it.

The Seventh of Adar—
THE DEATH ANNIVERSARY OF MOSES

The Zohar tells us that a righteous person or a kabbalist chooses the day he or she will leave this world. On the day of departure, all the Light that the righteous person revealed throughout his life is again revealed in a concentrated form. All this is described in detail with regard to Rav Shimon Bar Yochai, who not only chose the day he would leave the world, but also chose to return and be revealed every year on that same date. On this basis, Rav Shimon's death anniversary is considered a happy occasion. Unless they have studied Kabbalah, however, most people have difficulty accepting the idea that the death anniversary of a beloved person is not a sad and painful event. Yet Kabbalah enables us to celebrate the seventh of *Adar*, the anniversary of Moses' leaving the world. We sense the presence of Moses and express that feeling with happiness.

In order to connect to the special energy available at Moses' death anniversary, we read *The Zohar* portion of *Trumah*—a passage that discusses this issue. Moses left this world on the seventh of *Adar*, which takes place close to the week of the portion of *Trumah*. It is important to note that Rav Shimon composed *The Zohar* according to the chronological order of the Torah so as to reveal the Torah as a practical manual for understanding our true purpose in the world

In the modern world, every product comes with a user's manual. If I have a problem with my computer, I can readily turn to a page in the manual and find the solution to my problem. In a similar manner, if I have a problem in other areas of my life, I should look for an answer in *The Five Books of Moses*. There I will find solutions for literally all of life's problems. This may seem strange to those who are not familiar with Kabbalah; they may think that the Torah deals with a way of life that hasn't existed for thousand of years. The Torah seems like a history book, a book of poems, and a set of laws and ethical rules, with some occasional religious commentary. How, then, can the Torah be a practical user's manual? In fact, the Torah is a coded document whose hidden information must be deciphered—and the key to the code is *The Zohar*.

Therefore, without Kabbalah and *The Zohar*, there is no possibility of understanding the Torah. Only *The Zohar* can illuminate the Torah's hidden meaning. The Torah is like a sign on a highway at night—one that describes exactly where we should turn. But without our car's headlights, we will not be able to see the sign and will pass by without even noticing it. The same holds true of life as a whole: Without the Torah and *The Zohar* to illuminate it, we can never reach our life's destination.

With this in mind, let us return to the issue of Moses' death anniversary. "And we learned, said Rav Shimon, that Moses did not die," declares *The Zohar* (portion of *Trumah*, page 291, section 888). Here there would appear to be a contradiction between *The Zohar* and a clear statement in the Book of Deuteronomy regarding Moses' death. Indeed, Rav Shimon asks how it is possible to declare that Moses did not die when the Torah writes just the opposite. Therefore, Rav Shimon asks, "What is death?" He answers that death is only an illusion that looks real from our limited perspective: "But from the upper perspective, it is the opposite. Moses received more life." Moses' vitality increased in comparison to what it was in the physical body. *Miracles, Mysteries and Prayer*, a book published by The Kabbalah Centre, includes a detailed explanation of this concept.

The Zohar states that once a righteous person walks through the door to the afterworld, he or she is confronted with the revelation that death is merely an illusion. Unless one dies, there is no other way to really experience this truth. Death is the opening through which we can discover the truth about death. This is the answer to the seeming contradiction between *The Zohar* and The Bible. In the eyes of the Israelites, Moses died; he disappeared from their sight. But for himself, Moses still exists, free from the limitations of the physical body. Death is a function of consciousness: If we react only to what we see with our eyes, then the deceased are gone. But if we see beyond our physical senses, our understanding is infinitely deeper.

To the kabbalist, Moses is alive. The kabbalist can connect with Moses' raw energy, freed from any physical body, as a channel that downloads the Light of the Creator. But this is possible only as long as we agree in our consciousness with the idea of Moses' life beyond death. In the absence of this, we are like the Israelites at the time of the Golden Calf. The Israelites felt the need for the Golden Calf because they had disconnected from Moses, having assumed that Moses was dead and that he would no longer be capable of channeling the Light for them. They felt the need for an alternative channel of communication. They actually created a living calf from gold—not a simple statue, because they possessed the ability to dominate matter with their minds. They received this power from Moses on Mount Sinai, but they forgot that, as a result of the revelation on Mount Sinai, death was removed forever, and therefore Moses could not have died.

Moses is present with us now and calls on us to bring control over our lives.

There is no need to pray to an external God. Each one of us is a channel to reveal the Light force in the world. If we become pure channels, we will manifest God's ability to create miracles in our lives. Thus, *The Zohar* reveals that the

Israelites, not the Creator, caused the miracle of splitting the Red Sea. This wisdom has been hidden for 3,400 years, but in the Age of Aquarius the time has arrived to reveal it. Today we know how to connect to the consciousness of Moses. Moses wants to be with us, here and now. We accept the idea that he is alive, and as a result we will all merit life for ourselves.

Purim

What is the uniqueness of *Purim*? *Chanukah* (which occurs in the month of *Kislev*, the astrological sign of Sagittarius) and *Purim* (which falls in the month of *Adar*, the astrological sign of Pisces) are both ruled by the planet Jupiter. The genetic code of Jupiter connects it to the consciousness of miracles. When this planet was appointed to rule these months, it was established that Jupiter would become a channel to reveal the miracles of *Chanukah* and *Purim*.

In *The Book of Formation*, Abraham the Patriarch connected the month of *Adar* with the astrological sign of Pisces. The Aramaic word *Adar* means "special" or "unusual." What causes the month of *Adar* to be so special, and what is the connection between this uniqueness and the sign of Pisces?

Purim commemorates with happiness the fall of Haman. At *Chanukah* we celebrate a similar event, the victory of the *Maccabim* over the Greeks—but we don't say, "Once *Kislev* arrives we dwell in happiness." So there must be another explanation.

To find it, we must refer to the prayer known as the Ana Bekoach. Very few people are aware of this prayer, and even fewer know its meaning. The prayer consists of 42 words—seven verses of six words each. It describes the creation of the universe and everything that occurs within it. This information is embodied specifically in the first letters of each word, as a sequence of 42 Aramaic letters. All of Creation—all the stars and astrological signs, all that we encounter each day—is expressed in this one prayer, specifically in these 42 letters. The seven stars that influence our daily life are connected to the seven verses of this prayer. The second verse in the *Ana Bekoach* refers to the planet Jupiter, which controls the month of *Adar*.

This second verse contains a secret: Its chain of letters spells out the words *Krah Satan* קְרַע שָׂטָן (to tear away Satan). Everyone is advised to learn this chain by heart. These six letters that spell *Krah Satan* are connected to the month of *Adar*, as described by Abraham the Patriarch. Only through this combination of letters can we even dream of gaining control over our lives. Yet the combination works only during the months of *Adar* and *Kislev*, which are controlled by the planet Jupiter. This revelation starts on the eve of the first day of the month of *Adar* (*Erev Rosh Chodesh*

Adar). This is the seed level, which is the strongest aspect of any process.

In the month of *Adar*, there is an opportunity to exit the chaos that characterizes our lives today and to replace that chaos with control. Control in Kabbalah means complete removal of chaos from our lives. It means controlling our destiny in a manner that will fill our lives with happiness and health instead of sorrow and pain.

Historically, at *Chanukah* and *Purim*, a small group of people stood up to big empires and won. At *Purim*, the Israelites were destined to be destroyed by Haman, the second in command to King Achashverosh in Persia—but in the end it was Haman who was destroyed. It is important to note, however, that this victory did not take place because the enemy was attacked and defeated by an army. According to the teachings of Kabbalah, the real enemy is only consciousness. As with the war against the Greeks at *Chanukah*, the outcome was not decided on the battlefield. Instead, the war was against negative consciousness—the desire to receive for the self alone.

Haman was defeated because Haman's consciousness was defeated. How was this possible? Kabbalah teaches that a special battle strategy was successfully used at *Purim* against the root cause of chaos—against the thing that causes all physical or spiritual sickness, against the thing that brings the destruction of marriages and the failure of businesses. This is the mother of all wars: the Armageddon war between the consciousness of the Light and the desire to receive for the self alone. Kabbalah teaches that in the Age of Aquarius there will be a war of consciousness, because in this era we will understand that we must attack chaos at its source. That source is the desire to receive for the self alone.

Is it really possible to make fulfillment our reality and to end all pain and suffering? There are many superficial ways in which we can make ourselves happy, but once the bank manager calls and informs us about problems with our cash flow, all that happiness dissipates. How can we prevent these kinds of telephone calls? How can we prevent sorrow, lack, and pain in our lives? How can we fortify the drops of happiness spread throughout our lives and make them our dominant and continued reality? Only with *Krah Satan* in the month of *Adar*.

Although both occur under same astrological influences, there is an important difference between *Chanukah* and *Purim*. At *Chanukah*, a small group of people created the miracle; the multitudes did not participate. At *Purim*, in the month of *Adar*, all the Israelites participated in the fast as Esther asked of them. They took part in the successful journey that brought about the cancellation of Haman's consciousness.

When Mordechai returned from Jerusalem, it is written that he brought with him the knowledge of Kabbalah: all the letter combinations and all the holy names. He brought the system by which we can destroy negative consciousness. Mordechai and Esther, with the cooperation of all the

Israelites, erased negative consciousness from people's minds. Only in this way they were able to defeat the enemy; only in this way were they able to defeat Haman and everything Haman represented. That is why both the *Talmud* and *The Zohar* state that in the time of the Messiah, the only holiday we will celebrate will be *Purim*. By manifesting the energy of *Krah Satan* in the month of *Adar*, we have the opportunity to establish the power of immortality and to connect with the energy of the Messiah.

The Sabbath before *Purim* has a hidden aspect. Most people are not aware of this or don't give it much importance. We are referring to the reading of the portion of *Zachor* in addition to the regular reading. There is something special about this reading, and we are taught that it is important for women and children to participate and listen to it. This is not said about any other reading in the Torah.

Women, we learn from Kabbalah, have more positive energy than men. Only women, for example, have sufficient positive energy to bear children, which gives them the ability to connect with the portion of *Zachor* that is exceedingly positive in comparison to all other Torah portions. This is the story of *Amalek*, our antidote against doubt. We activate certainty within ourselves by listening to this reading so that we can harness the energy of certainty in our battle in the removal of doubt. What is the source of this power, and what is its connection to the holiday of *Purim*?

The context of the portion of *Zachor* appears in the Torah at the end of two portions: *Beshalach* and *Ki Tavo*. In the portion of *Beshalach*, there appears the secret of the awesome power of the 72 Names of God and the miracle of the splitting of the Red Sea. After witnessing those miracles, most people would be convinced that they could trust the Creator. The 72 Names of God enable us to achieve everything by connecting to the source of energy in the universe. But since the Israelites in the Sinai desert didn't practice restriction, they fell from the true world back to the world of illusion. Therefore they fell from the true world they had reached after splitting the Red Sea, and fell back into the world of uncertainty. In the physical world, in the illusory consciousness of uncertainty, we cannot connect to the present because we are constantly anxious about the unknown future. Fear is the handcuff that binds us to the illusion of the future and disconnects us from the present. If we truly connect to the present, we will have no doubt about the future because, according to the law of cause and effect, the present dictates the future.

The fruits of the Tree of Knowledge of Good and Evil represent illusory consciousness. The serpent did nothing but plant the seed of doubt in Eve. The serpent convinced her to exchange the consciousness of the true spiritual reality for the illusory consciousness of the physical world. Eve chose the physical world, and her consciousness made that choice an actuality.

As a result of not practicing restriction, the Israelites regressed to uncertainty, illusion, and doubt. But what is the connection between all this and *Purim*? Why is the reading of the portion of *Zachor* a condition to successful spiritual connection on *Purim*? And what spiritual force is revealed in the universe on this holiday?

At *Purim* we read *the Book of Esther* (*Megilat Esther*). In these Aramaic words, there is already a contradiction: *Megila* in Aramaic implies "revelation," and *Esther* is another way to say "concealment." The revelation of concealment is the consciousness of *Purim*. In *Purim*, the Light of *Chochmah*, which is concealed from us during the rest of the year, is finally revealed, and its revelation removes doubt, chaos, and any manifestation of negative energy in the entire universe. When Mordechai and Esther connected to this power 2,800 years ago, they, together with all the Israelites of the town of Shushan, created the miracle of *Purim*.

We don't celebrate *Purim* because we wish to commemorate the victory over Haman, but rather because of the energy that created the miracle of *Purim*. On the 13th day of *Adar*, we receive immediate certainty and immediate blessing—even more than we receive at *Yom Kippur*. In the month of *Tishrei*, we need to go through a whole process that ends only at *Sukkot*. At *Purim*, the revelation of Light is immediate. This day is a special cosmic occurrence that allows for the revelation of Light.

The importance of *Purim* and the cause for the huge revelation of Light that occurs on this holiday are connected to the immediate revelation of the concealed with *the Book of Esther*, and create a connection with the true world—a connection that promises the complete fulfillment of all our present needs and certainty about the future.

Kabbalah teaches that by removing doubt and uncertainty, we can banish chaos from the world. This is exactly what happens on *Purim*. The removal of the veil from the emanation of *Chochmah* enables us to connect immediately to the Light and to all the abundance it brings. In the time of the Messiah, all the holidays will be canceled except *Purim*, because the term *Messiah* means complete freedom from chaos, the cancellation of Murphy's Law, cancellation of the second law of thermodynamics, cancellation of the uncertainty principle, and the replacement of all these by complete and total certainty. Lack exists only where there is uncertainty. Therefore, resurrection of the dead in the time of the Messiah is not a revolutionary event, but a logical result of the canceling of the illusion of death.

What allowed the Israelites of Shushan, who were simple people, to connect to the world of truth? *The Book of Esther*, the removal of the veil over the emanation of *Chochmah*, and the revelation of the true world are what brought about this miracle. The *Talmud* teaches us that in the time of the Messiah, only the reality of *Purim* will exist, and all the Torah will be voided because it is no more than an illusory cover to true consciousness. The Torah's purpose is to enable us to receive in the illusory world. By reading stories about illusory events and by studying the hidden codes in them, we gain the key to the prison gate and are made capable of opening the gate and emerging from slavery to the illusion into the freedom of the true world. But when we connect to the true world, we will no longer need any tool to do so. Therefore, in the time of the Messiah, all the Torah will be canceled except the holiday of *Purim*, which will remain.

"There is, or there isn't" is the code to describe doubt, uncertainty, and illusory consciousness. The way to remove doubt is described in the Book of Moses, Aaron and Chor in the portion of *Zachor*, when they connected to the inner force of the letter *Bet* and established the system of the three columns in the spiritual world. By practicing restriction—by caring for others and loving our neighbors as ourselves—it is possible to gain blessing and certainty. Any description of the future that contains even a hint of negativity is necessarily a description of an illusion.

The concept of parallel realities, or two worlds—one of illusion and one of truth—answers many questions. We can transfer between the two worlds, just as we can transfer between programs working simultaneously on the computer. The illusory world was created to allow us to remove Bread of Shame. Only after we practice restriction in the illusory world can we have a taste of the true world. If we stop and give up, we return and fall back into the illusory world.

It is only recently that science has begun to discover the true world. As long as we deal with matter in terms of stone or iron, we are dealing with illusion. Only when we go down to the level of the single atom and penetrate the covering of the orbits is the truth revealed: The atom is only energy, a living and vibrating consciousness. The atom is mostly empty, and the solid nucleus holds an insignificant part of its volume. This is the true reality that *Purim* reveals to us. *Purim* reveals the structure of the atom and cancels the illusion of the tree and the metal. Reading *the Book of Esther* connects us to the certainty of the true world. It is the revelation of the concealed.

No one can complete correction, or achieve completeness by himself, with no help or cooperation from the people around him. We must all remember that we are part of the cosmic totality and must therefore have the desire to help all other aspects of the universe in order to achieve completeness. If all of us would remember that we need other people and that we must be willing to help all other human beings—a principle that is, in effect, the practical definition of the phrase "love your neighbor as yourself"—there would be no room for uncertainty. This is the essence of *Purim*. In no other holiday is there such a clear aspect of giving, cooperation, and caring for others. In *Chanukah* we give presents, but our activity is limited to the circle of our family, which is only an extended aspect of ourselves. Only in *Purim* is there a real giving to the other. Only in *Purim* is there a universal law to send presents.

Why only in *Purim* and not all through the year? Because during the year, the illusion of separation rules the world. Only in *Purim* is the mask removed and the truth revealed; only in *Purim* is the connection between all of Creation revealed by the presence of completeness.

The Torah was given to us for one purpose only: to remove the consciousness of the desire to receive for the self alone. The final destination is to achieve certainty, the elevation of the human consciousness, and liberation from mental and spiritual slavery.

When we read *the Book of Esther*, we not only reveal the secrets hidden within it but also build a connection to a cosmic event that occurs, according to The Ari, on this day alone. Only on *Purim* can we connect to the complete unity of the true world. In contrast to the holidays of the month of *Tishrei*, we don't have to spend days in the synagogue, we don't need a *Shofar* or a *Lulav*, and we don't need to fast or eat celery or honey. We don't even need to know anything—not even the difference between "blessed is Mordechai" and "cursed is Haman." Haman represents the dark side of us. We don't need a bulldozer to remove darkness in a room. It will suffice to light a match.

On *Purim* we are required to make only a very small effort. All we have to do is be happy and get drunk—and the drunker we become, the more complete will be the connection. In order to free ourselves from the hold of negativity in our lives, we need to free ourselves from the illusory world—

and the best way to do this on *Purim* is to get drunk. By losing our mindful consciousness, we remove the barrier that separates us from the cosmic consciousness. Since in *Purim* the entire cosmos is illuminated with the consciousness of certainty, by getting drunk on this day we gain certainty for the entire year. Drunkenness is not recommended on any other day of the year, since only on *Purim* is the universe full of certainty.

In order to remove the mental barrier, we use two tools: alcoholic beverages and *The Book of Esther*. *The Book of Esther* is so important that we will not merely sit and listen to it but will participate in it actively. Every time we read the name of Haman, we will meditate on the combination *Chaf-Hei-Taf* ת ה כ from The 72 Names of God, which is a ray of light, a laser beam that will remove the darkness named Haman. At the individual level, the thought of *Chaf-Hei-Taf* will remove any negativity caused by a negative thought or action. Only this combination of letters can do it. Therefore, it is best to keep quiet and concentrate during the reading. In about 40 minutes we will be able to achieve something that during the months of *Elul* and *Tishrei* takes us seven weeks of hard work. Whoever cannot dedicate themselves to this 40-minute period is surely deeply mired in the illusory world. Only a small effort is needed; one need not even read. It is enough to hear, as long as we concentrate and meditate on *Chaf-Hei-Taf* and maintain the correct consciousness.

At the time of the *Purim* miracle, complete love and caring existed among the Israelites. How can we connect to that energy today? Kabbalah teaches that this can happen only through knowledge and understanding. As long as there is no knowledge and understanding of the thing to which we want to connect, we have no chance of realizing the connection.

The Ari has written, "In order to continue that same shining of Mordechai and Rachel in *Purim* today, we give charity to the poor." Why? Because the word for charity in Aramaic צְדָקָה *tzedaka* comes from the Aramaic word for justice צֶדֶק *tzedek*. It is no accident that *Purim* occurs in the month of *Adar*. The planet controlling the month of *Adar* is Jupiter. By giving charity with love, we connect to the energy of Jupiter and the gifts to the poor closes the gaps in society and everyone becomes one soul in complete unity.

Many don't know that before *Purim*, Mordechai traveled to Israel. In the *Book of Nechemia* it is written, "These are the sons of the nation that came to Israel from the Diaspora caused by Nebuchadnetzar the King of Babylon, and they returned to Jerusalem and Judah each one to his city. The ones who came with Zrubabel were: Jeshua, Nehemia, Azariah, Raamiah, Nahamani, Mordecai, Bilshan, Misperth, Bigvai, Nehum, Baanah, the number of the people from the nation of Israel."

All these people went to Israel and stayed there. Only Mordechai returned to the Diaspora, to Shushan. Why did he do so? The answer lies in the *Talmud*, in the portion that deals with *the Book of Esther* and describes an amazing story related to Daniel the Prophet. Daniel also went to Persia, and he is buried there. The Persians nominated him to be the speaker on behalf of the rulers. Daniel was not a prophet, unlike Nechemia and Ezria from his generation, who are special for never having sinned in their entire lives.

In *the Book of Daniel*, portion 10, verse 7, it is written, "And I saw myself alone the mirror, and the people that were with me did not see the mirror . . ."

According to the *Talmud*, Daniel was at that time in the company of prophets, but only he saw the vision he described. The vision was accompanied by an earthquake that caused all the other prophets to run and hide. There is hardly any interpretation to this verse. What really happened there?

The Book of Daniel, like *The Zohar*, is written entirely in Aramaic. At that time, Aramaic was a spoken language in Persia. Hundreds of years after Daniel and Mordechai lived, Aramaic was the language in which *The Zohar* was revealed to Rav Shimon Bar Yochai. The entire Zohar came from *the Book of Daniel*. The purpose of Mordechai's trip to Israel and back was to connect to the knowledge of *The Zohar* and to bring this knowledge to Shushan. Mordechai taught them the power of *The Zohar*, by implementing this study in the form of unity and love for no reason, they established a connection that illuminated the world and defeated Haman. Unfortunately, not all those present at the Sin of the Golden Calf were present in the miracle of *Purim*. If each of them had been present in *Purim*, they would have corrected the damage done in the desert and would have revealed the Messiah then and there. The miracle of *Purim* in the presence of all the Israelites would have returned the world to a state of "death to death forever."

The "supporting actress" in this movie—the heroine of the story—was Esther, also known by the name *Hadassah*. Esther was a very special prophet. She controlled, by herself, all the events of *Purim*. She caused the victory without force of any kind. It is true that all the Israelites supported her spiritually, but physically she worked alone in the royal palace.

Why are we told that Esther is also called *Hadassah*? As we know, the strength of the Israelites is not measured in physicality, but as the strength of the connection to the 72 Names of God. They will never win their enemies by physical strength alone but will do so only with the power of the *Chaf-Hei-Taf* combination, which Esther transferred to Mordechai via Daniel. Daniel received the message in Aramaic and passed it to Mordechai, who then spread it among all the Israelites of Shushan. This is the message we have the merit to study today in the form of Kabbalah. The name Hadassah comes from the Aramaic word *Hadas* (myrtle)—the same plant we use for our connection on *Sukkot*, in the *Havdalah* every Saturday night, under the *Chuppah* (canopy) at a wedding, and at the *Brit Milah* (circumcision). This plant is unique because its leaves grow in bunches of three from one joint point. The power of the *Hadas* lies in the power of completion and unity of the three-column system.

When we read *the Book of Esther* with the help of the knowledge we received from Daniel through Rav Shimon, we establish the three-column system. We will draw into the entire world the light of the Messiah, and we will cancel completely any revelation of chaos from the universe. With the help of this knowledge, we can accomplish the destiny of *the Book of Esther*: We can reveal the concealed, which is the inner force in the 72 Names of God, especially the combination of *Chaf-Hei-Taf*. With the help of this combination, we will defeat Haman, which represents all the negative intelligent energy in the universe—because Haman can be defeated only with the power of the Light, not with physical strength.

The importance of Esther and *the Book of Esther*, as well as the uniqueness of *Purim*—that which puts it in a completely separate category from *Rosh Hashanah*, *Yom Kippur*, *Sukkot*, *Pesach*, and *Shavuot*—is explained by the *Talmud*: "Do and accept what has been accepted already." But perhaps we might ask, How is it possible that *the Book of Esther*, which was written by a human being, was more important than the Torah given to us by the Creator Himself? The answer hides in the explanation to a verse from the *Talmud*. At *Purim*, the Israelites accepted and practiced in actuality the Torah given on Mount Sinai—something they had not done 600 years previously during the event at Mount Sinai. That is where the Torah was given, and only on *Purim* was it received by the Israelites. This is the uniqueness of *Purim*, and this is the secret of its importance. As long as the Israelites didn't accept the Torah, it was as if the Torah didn't even exist for them, and therefore all the laws and holidays that emanated from it have a limited and temporary importance only. For 2,800 years, the Israelites held the key to a huge revelation that, unlike the Torah, will remain forever.

How can we achieve this? By studying Kabbalah. There we learn why Daniel was called *Hatach* הֲתָךְ : to teach us that everything in *the Book of Esther* was coded. There we learn why Esther was not content with merely canceling Haman's decree, but she canceled the evil plot that Haman planned against Israel from the root and the entire world. Esther focused on the cause level of all the chaos in the world—not on the physical being of people, but on the thoughts of hatred that passed in their minds on their way to manifestation in the world. If we rid ourselves of Haman and not of the energy that causes people to think thoughts of hate, then we would not have done anything, and another terrorist would immediately rise and continue from where Haman left off. We destroyed many enemies, but we didn't bring everlasting peace to the world. *The Book of Esther* is a tool for the complete defeat of the negative powers in the world, forever.

In closing, let's now give some attention to the other protagonist in the *Purim* story: the evil Haman. Haman knew that if he succeeded in blocking the flow of Light on the night of the 14th of *Adar*, it would be the end of Israel, because this Light is not revealed on any other day of the year. Haman also knew that if he failed, the Diaspora would end and he would not be able to stop the revelation of Light in the world. This leads us to the most outrageous declaration The Ari ever made. Until this point, we described Haman as the villain in the story. But Haman was a person too, just like Abraham and Isaac. Like them, he was a chariot —a channel through which was revealed a certain intelligent thought energy, a kind of consciousness, a certain energy essence.

Animals don't ask questions. Humans, on the other hand, can and must ask questions to try to attain an understanding and purpose to their actions. Blind following of commands is not human and serves only those whose consciousness is limited to the illusory, physical world. God never intended to say—and never said—that we must obey without asking questions. The attitude of commandments is idol worshipping. The enemy of the Israelites, therefore, is anyone who brings a religious approach that forbids questions—anyone who says, "Because it is written."

All those who support the religious way are responsible for the chaos in the world and are delaying the Messiah. The defeat of Haman was achieved by simple people who raised questions without fear—and by Mordechai and Daniel, who brought from Jerusalem the knowledge to answer this question. The Ari tells us that the only holiday that will remain at the end of time is *Purim*. Why will only *Purim* remain forever? The reason is that for 2,000 years, the true meaning of the word Messiah was misunderstood. The Ari explains that the Messiah is a kind of energy that shines on the universe and removes any aspect of negativity completely.

In the time of the Messiah, every day will be *Purim*, because the consciousness of *Purim* is the consciousness of the Messiah. There will be total removal of chaos, pain and suffering from the world forever. The Messiah and *Purim* are one and the same.

Rosh Chodesh Nissan
(ARIES)

In *The Book of Formation*, composed by Abraham the Patriarch, it is written: "He crowned the letter *Hei* and formed by it the ram in the world and the month of *Nissan* in the year and the right hand in the soul, male and female."

The letter *Hei* ה (the fifth letter in the Aramaic alphabet), is the DNA of the sign of Aries and the month of *Nissan*. Its inner consciousness is also their inner consciousness. What is the reason this letter is connected to the month of *Nissan*, the beginning of the year? The explanation is found in the Torah, in the portion of *Lech Lecha*. There the Creator changes Abram's name to Abraham in order for him to become fertile, to experience a breakthrough and transform him into the father of a huge nation. For the same reason, Sarah's name was changed from Sarai to Sarah. The inner energy of the letter *Hei* allows for the occurrence of miracles and wonders and the mind ruling over matter. This is the energy that made it possible for Sarah to conceive and give birth to Isaac at the age of 90. This is the energy that made possible the Exodus from Egypt, the ten plagues, and the parting of the Red Sea.

When we read biblical stories, we do not focus on their historical aspect but rather on their hidden spiritual meaning. Since the letter *Hei* is capable of creating miracles, it is situated in the first month of the year—the seed level of the entire year. From there it can give us control over our destiny and life for the entire year.

Whoever thinks the reason for Passover is to commemorate the exodus from physical slavery to physical freedom, or to provide a reason for a yearly family reunion, is totally wrong. The Torah does not leave any room for misinterpretation: Every time the Israelites met with any difficulty during their travels in the Sinai desert, they turned to Moses and demanded that he return them to Egypt. Slavery in Egypt was not physical, but rather a slavish addiction to the desire to receive for the self alone. The Torah makes it clear that the Exodus and everything related to it was forced on the Israelites, including the giving of the Torah on Mount Sinai.

The ancient Egyptians knew how to enslave people using negative consciousness. The addiction to the desire to receive for the self alone is the cause and root of the Diaspora. On the 15th day of the month of *Nissan*, there is a revelation of a force that makes it possible to break free from the addictions, to build a complete spiritual vessel. This is the code that can change the world from chaos and transform sorrow to order and harmony. Just as the physical DNA is composed of different combinations of amino acids, so too is the spiritual DNA formed of different combinations of the Aramaic alphabet. The letter *Hei* has the power to impose the consciousness of mind over matter. With the letter *Hei*, the water of the Nile can be changed from water to blood and back to water. But it is not enough to know the letter *Hei*; we must also recognize the schedule of cosmic programs. The Creator wants to assist us, but since our decision prior to the first restriction, the Creator restricts this beneficence to specific, rhythmic periods. If we pray at the wrong time, our prayers cannot be accepted, even though the Creator hears and wants to answer them.

For the first time in history, we have the all the information we need to create change in the cosmos: both the meditations that accompany the prayer and the schedule of cosmic events. On the night of Passover, using the new prayer books and with the support of all the people using them all over the world, we have a chance. It is important to remember that the removal of chaos is directly connected to breaking the chains of addiction—transforming the desire to receive for the self alone to the desire to receive for the sake of sharing. We manifest this transformation by having consideration and sensitivity to the needs of others. We live in the era of which *The Zohar* says, "Woe to those who will live in that era, and praise to those who will live in that era."

Human behavior will dictate whether this month will be a seed for bloodshed, God forbid, or for the elevation and correction of the soul. On the night of Passover, we gain the power to instill order on our lives and remove the chaos. But we will not be able to materialize this gift as long as we harbor hatred in our lives. For those who cannot relinquish hate, neither the connection nor all the lessons described in this book will help.

But does this mean that we should lose all personal characteristics and think alike? No, everyone must maintain his uniqueness, and with the same conviction must strive to maintain his friends' ideas even if they are different. This is the union of differences. This is the way to restrict and reveal Light in the world. The filament in a light bulb allows the flow of electricity through restriction, and the result is revelation of light and the removal of darkness. Once we reveal the Light of the Creator in our lives, any aspect of darkness, chaos, destruction, and Satan consciousness will disappear.

During the month of *Nissan*, we must expect arguments and conflicts, which are simply opportunities to reveal Light. The negative side will do everything in its power to cause us to react inconsiderately, and in this way prevent us from using the tools we have at our disposal to control our destiny. But we will not be trapped; we shall elevate and confront the responsibility entrusted to us, bringing peace to the world and putting an end to any violent conflict. We have a duty to turn on the Light, and whoever is not capable of loving the enemy should at least act with human dignity toward him.

The reason is very simple. In the month of *Nissan*, it is possible to end the era of suffering, to change the face of the world, and to bring order, peace, and love.

Pesach
(PASSOVER)

As with all other holidays, we do not celebrate *Pesach* because of tradition or religious belief. Rather, Passover is a cosmic code that gives us an understanding of truths that lie beyond the reach of our five senses—truths from the spiritual realm, which contains 99.9999% of reality. Without understanding this, we cannot understand the world in which we live. Kabbalah teaches that there is an all-knowing cosmic intelligence that includes and embraces the entire energy of the cosmos. If I want to know what will happen tomorrow, I can connect to the cosmic intelligence and gain the knowledge I need because tomorrow already exists within that intelligence.

Naturally, everyone would like to know what the future holds for them. Imagine the ramifications of this capability to a stockbroker! But we are interested in spiritual achievements, not merely with the acquisition of successful stocks. Success in the stock market cannot guarantee happiness, health, longevity, harmony, or good relationships, all of which are accomplished using the tools and wisdom of Kabbalah.

Passover occurs in the month of *Nissan*, when the ruling planet is Mars and the astrological sign is Aries. As explained previously, Jerusalem is not holy because the Temple was built there, but rather the Temple was built there because Jerusalem is connected to holy energy. A manifestation in the physical realm can never be the cause. This is also true of the timing of Passover. The historic events of Passover took place about 2,400 years ago, but those events must be the result of other events that took place at the time of Creation. In other words, we must look at Passover as a result of the universe rather than seeing the universe as a result of Passover.

Passover always occurs in the spring, during the month of *Nissan*, when the astrological sign of Aries influences the universe in conjunction with the planet Mars. Passover will never be more than a few days away from March 31, which is the first day of spring. Rav Isaac Luria, The Ari, explains that it is written in *the Book of Exodus*, "This month is to you the head of all months, the first to you of all the months of the year." What is the significance of the words "to you"? During the Exodus from Egypt, everyone was given the ability to control the cosmic code for the first time in history. Before this time, only a chosen few—Adam, Abraham, Isaac, and Jacob—knew the secrets of the universe. At the time of the Exodus, however, this knowledge became available to everyone. "To you" this means that the knowledge and technology of spiritual communication and the control of destiny were given to the Israelites on behalf of future generations for the benefit of all humankind. In effect, the responsibility and duty to use this information was given "to you"—that is, to all the Israelites.

The Israelites went down to Egypt in order to connect to negativity and to remove Bread of Shame, which is achieved by restricting at the right moment when the opportunity presents itself. The Israelites could control the movies of their lives. They could fast-forward, rewind, or change the tape altogether! We need to know that tapes can be replaced and that other tapes exist. We need to have the ability to read the labels on the tapes in order to choose a desirable one from those available. But first we need to know that such an opportunity exists and when it is scheduled to occur.

The optimal time to remove negativity is when the desire to receive for the self alone reaches its high point, which happens during the month of *Nissan*—when Mars, the planet of war, influences the world though the sign of Aries. Aries symbolizes the pioneer that leads the way, and it is fortified by the power it gets from Mars—the same power that is also responsible for the spring. By controlling the force of Mars, we can control the power of growth and rejuvenation in our lives, just as nature does in spring. Living in chaos with a lack of control is like living in prison. We can crack the walls of the prison cell at Passover and be free because the occasion affords us an opportunity to activate restriction over the desire to receive for the self alone.

Specifically, at Passover we can reveal the positive side of Mars, which is the power of rejuvenation. Mars is the planet of war. The desire to receive for the self alone is always the cause of any war. Mars is the channel for this consciousness, as it is responsible for the illusion of separation that prevents people from seeing the quantum connection between things. This consciousness is responsible for the physical proximity between Mars and earth, the realm of *Malchut*. The ram that appeared at Isaac's sacrifice is the ram that is revealed in the spring—the symbol of selfish desire. For this reason, Abraham the Patriarch made the connection between the sign of Aries and the planet Mars. Both represent the same consciousness—that of the desire to receive for the self alone—and both connect to the energy of judgment. The world's center of judgment is in Egypt. That is the reason the Egyptians chose the ram as their god. The Egyptians understood that spiritual reality determines the events of the physical world. They recognized the power of Aries and knew that its consciousness is manifested in the physical world through the ram. They didn't worship the animal itself, but rather the spiritual energy it represents. The Egyptians knew how to connect to the energy of the cosmic sign of Aries through the ram, and through Aries they controlled the revelation of judgment in the world.

Aviv is the Aramaic word for spring. This word can be separated into two syllables: *Av* אָב (father) and *Iv* יָב (in Aramaic, the numerical value of 12). Spring is the first of the 12 months and the father of all the months, which is why Aries is the first sign in the Zodiac. On the first day of the month of *Nissan*, we witnessed—for the first time in the history of mankind—a whole nation united in the understanding and practice of the three-column system. The slaughter of the ram represented the activation of the power of restriction over the desire to receive for the self alone, which was the essence of Egyptian culture. The Israelites gained the strength they needed for this breakthrough from the positive aspect of the sign of Aries and the planet Mars. This act changed their movie and made possible the Exodus from Egypt. During the holidays of the lunar month of *Tishrei*, we receive a year's life extension on our contract. In the month of *Nissan*, we can change our way of life and correct the rest of the year accordingly.

It is true that one can repent on any day of the year, but at *Nissan* there is cosmic assistance. *Nissan* enables us to bring about change at the root level—from the seed—from the first month of the year. The Israelites received the precept of blessing the new moon before the plague of the firstborn, at the root level. After having attained control over the month of *Nissan*, they could easily cope with this plague—the cosmic event of removing selfish desire at its root level—by causing the Angel of Death to pass over the Israelites' houses during the plague of the firstborn. The name of the holiday derives from this fact. If we can establish spiritual consciousness during the holiday of Passover, chaos will pass us and we shall achieve Messiah. If we do not do so, God forbid, the opportunity of the holiday will skip us.

We should familiarize ourselves with the physical "hardware" of Passover. By understanding this hardware, we may establish the power of connection. (With the help of The Ari, we will discover the Passover *Hagaddah* or connection book, which is the software compatible with the Passover hardware.) All vegetation is connected to the three-column system, which is why plants renew and grow in the spring. We too have the opportunity to choose to connect in the spring, when the universe is flooded with the energy of life, renewal, and freedom from the restraints of our old movies. By preparing a suitable spiritual vessel, it is possible for us to harness the spring's energy blast in a balanced way and to reveal tremendous Light in the world. The Aramaic calendar matched the lunar year with the solar year in order to connect Mars, Aries, and the month of *Nissan*. Only this combination can supply the boost of energy needed to break the chains of destiny—to change the movie and to attain freedom from chaos. The Exodus from Egypt was the result of this special date, which we call Passover *Pesach*.

More than any other nation in history, the Egyptians connected to the desire to receive for the self alone. Since this desire is the essence of the physical world, this connection is the key to controlling matter. This is the power the Egyptians used to build the Pyramids, and to this day, no one has been able to duplicate their material accomplishments.

How did they do it? The selfish desire breaks the circle of connection that unites all creation and fosters the illusion of separation, space, and linear time. Whoever is under the influence of the selfish desire sees himself as disconnected from the rest of the universe. He can see only one point, which is himself. For this reason, he is disconnected from the origin of the cosmic force that can free him from the robotic slavery to destiny and reactive behavior.

By practicing restriction of selfish desire—by controlling this desire and transforming it into a desire to share—anyone can be freed from the chains of illusion and connect to the reality that unites past, present, and future and ties the individual to the rest of the universe. This tie gives us the power to break the chains of our destiny, and it is the key to freedom. In order to defeat the Egyptian nation, the Israelites first had to convert their selfish desire into the desire to receive for the sake of sharing. This transformation was achieved with the blessing of the new moon and through the slaughter of the ram.

During the first night of Passover, and only during the first night, the universe is free from the chains of destiny. Only on this night can we access the cosmic assistance needed to change and replace our movie for a better one without having to be completely righteous human beings. Anyone can use this opportunity to activate the software in the book of connection, the *Hagaddah*, in order to draw spiritual abundance from the hardware that is available at that time in the universe. Anyone can change his movie as if with a magic wand and break free from preordained destiny. This is the whole secret of Passover.

The Ari explains that before any redemption can occur, it is necessary to go down into the mud of physical difficulty in order to earn purification. This was the situation of the Israelites at the time of the Exodus, with the significant difference that the Israelites had become addicted to the "mud." Even when Moses promised them the 72 Names of God and the Torah—the tools with which they could connect to wells of cosmic energy and draw endless abundance to themselves and the whole world—they kept complaining about what they had left behind in Egypt.

Think of it! If I offered you $50 million, would you also ask for a free tape recorder? It doesn't make sense. When the Israelites were freed, they didn't realize that they would have to manifest their potential by actually restricting. The Creator literally forced this redemption on them. If the Israelites had reached a lower level of negativity, they could not have been saved. They would not have been able to activate the power of restriction to remove selfish desire and negative consciousness.

Kabbalah teaches that every event in the universe is the result of human action. If we are good or bad, we create a positive or negative energy that is the cause of all phenomena. This is exactly what Kabbalah states, even if we don't see the correlation between cosmological events and human actions. If we want to control future events, we must control the tape we are transmitting. We decide what will be realized from endless possibilities. From the moment we insert the tape and turn on the cosmic appliance, the order of events is imposed in a strict manner, without any free will. But by using restriction, we can eject the tape, choose a different one from the endless variety, and insert the new tape in place of the old. On the night of the *Seder* (meal of order), we can change our movie for the following year until next Passover. Every person's first tape is decided according to acts from previous lifetimes. As long as people do not take action to change their first movie, their script will remain the same year after year, and their future will be predictable. But on the night of the *Seder*, we are given the opportunity to change the future. *The Zohar* states that every person who connects to the Light revealed on the night of the *Seder* will be transported to a parallel universe and will connect to a tape from which all judgments from past lives will be erased. This is the opportunity that the holiday of Passover offers us, and we shouldn't miss it.

The 10th day of the month of *Nissan* is called the *Shabbat Hagadol* (Big Shabbat). On this day, the Creator revealed again the force of *Zeir Anpin*, the which until that moment was in a fetal state. This enormous revelation of Light is the basis of this special *Shabbat*. The revelation of Light allowed the Israelites, for the first time in history, to take control over the desire to receive for the self alone. Previously, only a chosen few—such as Abraham, Isaac, and Jacob—were able to do so. But on the Big Shabbat, the whole nation united against the desire to receive for the self alone.

That is why on this day, the Israelites were told to bring a ram into their homes and then to bind it and prepare it for slaughtering as a Passover sacrifice. Controlling the ram blocked the energy that sustained Egypt. This is the purpose of the Big Shabbat: It paves the way to the Exodus. If the Israelites had not learned to control the ram, Passover could not have occurred. In order to manifest a thought energy, we must take action in the physical realm. The physical control over the ram during the Big Shabbat manifested the spiritual control over the desire to receive for the self alone and enabled the revelation of the Light of *Zeir Anpin* in the world.

When the Israelites were facing the Red Sea, they turned to the Creator and asked for help. And what was the Creator's answer? "Why do you call to me?" *The Zohar* explains that this was not a time for praying, but rather a time for action—a time to control physical matter through the power of consciousness. In order to do this, however, we need to fulfill three prerequisites: first, total belief that we can manifest such control; second, the correct use of the holy names, such as the 72 Names of God that connect consciousness and matter; and third, an understanding that only through the Light of the Creator can control over matter be achieved and channeled through us to the world. These three prerequisites were activated at the time of the splitting of the Red Sea. The controlling consciousness was "Water—move to the sides. Mud at the bottom of the sea—harden and become smooth and as easy to cross as a paved road."

Even if we have total certainty and pure consciousness, we still need a transformer that can transfer our thought energy to matter. This is the purpose of the 72 Names of God that were used during the splitting of the Red Sea, as described in the portion of *Beshalach*, verses 19-21. It is not we who make miracles, but the Light of the Creator that is behind every thought. The Light, which is within us always, can be revealed only through and by us. Only we can decide how the Light of the Creator will be revealed in the world. This is the reason for the Creator's answer: "Why do you scream to me?"

Can we decide, therefore, to walk through a wall or to travel to Tokyo in one minute? What's stopping us? Only the illusion of space and time, which is filled with negative consciousness, prevents us from moving in space freely. In order to cancel this blockage, we need to remove negativity and replace it with Light.

CHAMETZ

The checking for *chametz* and its removal is an important Passover concept. This is done the night before the holiday starts, on the 14th of *Nissan*. We first distribute ten pieces of bread around the house, and we then collect and burn them. Today, people often confuse searching for the *chametz* and ordinary spring cleaning. This is a confusion between inner, spiritual order and physical tidiness. Searching for the *chametz* is a matter of inner cleansing, which is needed as preparation for the holiday. Conquering the selfish desire, represented by the *chametz* consciousness, is necessary to ensure that the Light revealed on the night of the *Seder* will promote our correction process and will not be transferred to the negative side. Actually, there is no need to clean all the physical *chametz* from the house. In the blessing we recite at the time of checking, we declare that any *chametz* we miss is not to be considered. What is important is the cleansing of our inner selfish desire, not the cleaning of bread crumbs. As we remove the *chametz* in the evening, we awaken the inner spiritual process of soul searching. We remember all the times we behaved in hurtful ways toward others. By this inner cleansing, we prepare the spiritual vessel to download the software that will make it possible for us to connect to the Light, and to correct the entire year from its root level.

The burning of the *chametz* the next morning brings an end to the desire to receive for the self alone and kills the Angel of Death within us. For this reason, we burn the Passover sacrifice and scorch a chicken throat to place on the *Seder plate*. The searching and burning of the *chametz* is the base on which we install the software for the night of the *Seder*. It is a resurrection of the soul (in the *Neshamah* level) from the prison in which it has been confined—a prison of materialistic consciousness and selfish desire. The burning of the *chametz* erases this negative consciousness in preparation for the reading of the *Hagaddah* and the reinstallation of the software that can produce a new movie of our lives.

The Seder Plate

The arrangement of the *Seder Plate* (see Diagram 5) is the first step in the process of installing the software. The Aramaic word for the *Seder Plate* is *Kearah* קְעָרָה, which has a numerical value of 375, or 365 + 10. By preparing a clean vessel containing the Ten *Sfirot* (Emanations) at the time of the checking of the *chametz*, we gain control over the coming 365 days. The plate itself represents the *Sfirah* of *Malchut*, the physical world. So far we have been preparing ourselves to connect with the Light. Now, however, we are dealing with tools that draw the Light and direct it to us. When we are in the right consciousness, we can use the *Seder Plate* to connect to the energy revealed that night. This is not religion or tradition; it is a spiritual journey beyond space and time into a parallel universe and a better world—and the *Seder Plate* is the spaceship that can transport us on that journey.

There are two ways to arrange the *Kearah*: one according to The Ari, and the other according to the Gaon of Vilna. We at The Kabbalah Centre arrange it according to The Ari. On the plate we place seven objects, representing *Chesed-Gvurah-Tiferet*, *Netzach-Hod-Yesod*, in the form of the Shield of David: two triangles, one on top of the other. At the top right, the place of Chesed, we put a scorched chicken throat representing the scorched ram *(Z'roah)* from the original Passover sacrifices. The scorching of the ram destroyed the consciousness of desire for the self alone that the ram channeled. After the consciousness of the left side has been scorched and destroyed, only the right column remains. This is the consciousness of *Chesed*, so the scorched throat is placed at the point that matches the emanation of *Chesed*. If we were to burn the throat completely, we would destroy its right side as well, so we scorch it only through use of the correct consciousness.

At the upper left of the Plate, corresponding to the emanation of *Gvurah*, we put a hard-boiled egg. In Aramaic, the word for egg is *Beitzah*, which also means "desire." This is no coincidence. In Gate of Meditations, The Ari reveals that the ruling consciousness of the egg is the left column, the desire to receive. When the egg is cooked, this consciousness becomes stronger. When cooked, the egg hardens while other foods soften. This act of hardening the desire to receive for the self alone is associated with Pharaoh.

In the lower middle area of the Plate, for the emanation of *Tiferet*, we place bitter herbs and horseradish, known in Aramaic as *Maror*. In Gate of Meditations, The Ari has written, "And the *Maror* has a similar numerical to *Mavet* (death), and it has the aspect of hard judgments." *Gematria*, numeric value, or numerology, is Kabbalah's way of expressing mathematical equations. When we taste a spoon of minced horseradish, we immediately have a taste of death. But if we restrict and continue chewing it, the taste changes and becomes sweet. As The Ari describes it, "They have to be minced and chewed to sweeten their bitterness." This is a real precept: In order to reveal the Light of life and rejuvenate, we must kill the desire to receive for the self alone and activate restriction. When we taste bitterness, we feel a strong desire to calm it with bread or water. But when we restrict this impulse, we kill the selfish desire and reveal balanced Light.

The paradox of restricting what we want most, and the balance achieved as a result, are both connected to central-column consciousness. Another way to understand the connection between the power of restriction and the center column is to see the restriction as the cover, which reveals and separates entities. Without identification and distinction, things would be mixed into a single substance, as in the first vessel before the original restriction. By the force of restriction, it is possible to separate and identify the different entities, to manifest each potential, and to create harmony among them.

In the right lower area of the Plate, corresponding to the emanation of *Netzach*, we put a sweet fruit blend called *Haroset*. As The Ari explains in *The Gate of Passover*, "And the secret of the *Haroset* is a hint of clay, in the secret of Leah, and we have to sweeten her judgments too." The Aramaic word for clay is *tit* טיט. Its numerical value is 28, the same as the Aramaic word for strength *koach* כח. So the Haroset gives us strength, but strength for what? According to *The Zohar*, Leah is the code name of the female aspect of the upper triangle: the potential, hidden aspect of the Shield of David. The female side is also connected to judgment. With the *Haroset*, we can sweeten the judgment in the secret of Leah.

The *Haroset* contains ten ingredients, consisting of seven fruits and three roots—wine, apples, almonds, different nuts, dates, persimmon, figs, ginger, cumin, and clove. The three roots represent the emanations of *Keter-Chochmah-Binah*. The fruits are the lower seven emanations. The fruits and roots are channels to the energy of the emanations in the form of returning Light. By elevating returning Light, we can sweeten judgments and facilitate the manifestation of resurrection and immortality.

In the Plate's lower left area—the emanation of *Hod*—we place a piece of parsley, *Karpas*. This contains the word *parek?* (meaning hard work, or oppression) and the letter *Samech*. The descent to Egypt involved hard work and oppression, but all problems and difficulties in life are meant to purify us. Pressure is what differentiates a piece of coal from a diamond. The complete certainty in the Light's purpose, whose only desire is to bestow good upon us, is the essence of the emanation of *Hod*.

In the lower middle area of the Plate, the emanation of *Yesod*, we put lettuce, which in Aramaic is called *Chasah*. The word *Chasah* contains *chas* (mercy), which the emanation of *Yesod* gives to *Malchut*. In the same way, Joseph showed mercy to his brothers when they were reunited, despite all they had done to him in their youth.

The three *Matzot* placed next to the Plate are for the upper three emanations, and together with the lower seven areas of the plate they complete the representation of the ten emanations. The three *Matzot* represent *Keter-Hochmah-Binah*, or the right, left, and center columns. They are also known by the code names Cohen, Levy, and Israel. The upper *Matza*, called Cohen, acts as the channel to the energy intelligence of the Endless. The second *Matza*, Levy, elevates the desire to receive for the self alone. The lower *Matza*, called Israel, elevates the center-column energy and connects to the revelation of the endless Light. The *Matzot* are connected to the right column because they have changed their consciousness. The basic consciousness of dough is similar to the ram's consciousness—one of ego and selfish desire. By revealing the power of restriction during the special baking, the dough is prevented from absorbing liquids and rising. This represents the elimination of the selfish desire that existed in the dough. What remains in the *Matza* is right-column consciousness: humility and caring for others.

This process of transformation from selfish desire to desire to share makes possible the revelation of endless Light in our lives. This is the inner essence of Passover. Mars, the planet of war, blood, and death, controls *Nissan*. But blood is also the soul and life. By freely choosing the process of transformation based on the power of restriction, we reveal completion in the month of *Nissan*, an actual revelation of Messiah consciousness.

THE HAGADDAH

The keyboard on our Passover computer is the *Hagaddah*, the Passover connection book. In this keyboard there are 15 keys. Each one activates another level in the computer program that brings order and redemption to the world. The name of the levels are *Kadesh, Urchatz, Karpas, Yachatz, Magid, Rachtzah, Motzi, Matza, Maror, Korech, Shulchan Orech, Tzafun, Barech, Halel, and Nirtzah.* Through meditation on these stages, and through the Ten *Sfirot* represented on the plate and the *Matzot*, we can connect to the power of Passover if we fulfill two conditions. First, we must recognize the internal cosmic paradox: In order to receive we must first restrict. Second, as we sit around the *Seder* table, we must understand the wider cosmic meaning of Passover. On the night of the *Seder*, we must make a personal decision that from this moment forward, we will make every possible effort to convert the negative energy inside us to positive energy. In order to achieve this transformation, we must take advantage of every opportunity to restrict. In order to remove negativity from within us, we must fill ourselves with Light. This is exactly what happens to those with the right consciousness on the night of the *Seder*.

1. Let us now look at the *Kiddush*, the blessing over the wine, and at *Kadesh*, which is the first blessing over the wine and the first step in the *Seder*. This blessing connects us to Holiness—*Kedusha*. It connects us to completeness, to all-inclusive harmony, and to endless life. We use red wine

because it has the ability to draw Light and represents the desire to receive. But the way in which the *Kiddush* is made prevents the Light from accumulating within us. Instead, the *Kiddush* creates an endless flow of Light that passes through us, nourishes us, and continues to flow, connecting us in a circle of energy with all of Creation. During the *Seder*, we drink wine four times for a total of four cups. In this first step—the *Kadesh*—we drink the first cup, which nourishes us with the energy of the letter *Yud* and connects us to the *Sfirah*, the emanation of *Chochmah*.

2. *Urechatz*. In this step, only the Head of the Table washes his hands. He does this meditating to do it for everyone present. We use our hands to give and receive, to create and destroy. Through them, we reveal Light in our lives. But since negativity is attracted to any revelation of Light, it attaches itself to the tips of our fingers. By washing the hands with the energy of mercy (*Chesed*), which is transferred to the physical world through water, we neutralize the negative influence. In this way, it is prevented from attaching itself to the Light revealed during the meal.

3. *Karpas*. Using the parsley, we connect to the *Sfirah* of *Hod*, the representation of the left column on the upper triangle of *Zeir Anpin*. We dip the parsley in salt water, representing positive consciousness, in order to balance it. The salt is an important mineral for sustaining life, as its positive energy can also balance the desire to receive in the bread. In the same way, we use the salt to balance the parsley. We dip the parsley in the salt, make the blessing for vegetables, and

eat it. This blessing (*Bore Pri Ha-adama*) also includes the bitter herbs we eat later in the *Seder*. As we know, everything in the world has a physical aspect and a spiritual aspect. The physical aspect is connected to the desire to receive for the self alone. This connection to the spiritual aspect is achieved with a spiritual tool: the blessing over the food.

4. *Yachatz*. The Head of the Table takes the middle *Matza*, called the Levy, and breaks it into two parts. The middle *Matza* is the representation of the letter *Hei* of the Tetragrammaton, the *Sfirah* of *Binah*. The upper *Matza* represents the letter *Yud* and the *Sfirah* of *Chochmah*, and the lower *Matza* is the letter *Vav*—the *Zeir Anpin*. We represent the *Malchut*, the last *Hei* in the Tetragrammaton, and we complete this system with our physical bodies.

The middle *Matza* is connected to the letter *Hei*, which has two parts: the letter *Dalet* and the letter *Vav*. Before breaking the *Matza*, we connected it to the left column through the emanation of *Binah*. The consciousness of the *Matza* now goes through another transformation: The smaller part of the two will be connected to the letter *Dalet* and the word *Dal* (or poor). The Exodus, which freed the people of Israel, was not something that the Israelites deserved. They were poor in both a spiritual and an energetic level. They didn't gain this merit by their own doing. Instead, God showered them with his benevolence and released them from darkness. We contemplate all this when we look at the small part of the middle *Matza*.

Breaking the *Matza* is like splitting the atom. Our thoughts about poverty will connect us to the empty spaces in the atom, the nonphysical part that makes up most of its volume. The purpose of this meditation is to remind us that the Light we receive on the night of the *Seder* and during the entire seven days of Passover comes to us by the goodness of the Creator, not by our own merit. We don't merit any of the holiday's benefits. Do we, in fact, even merit all the knowledge that is revealed to us, including the explanations by Rav Shimon and The Ari regarding the consciousness and the significance of the holidays? What is the difference between us and all the others who didn't have the opportunity to learn these things for 2,000 years? We must remember that we are no better than all the other generations; we didn't earn this tremendous merit. Everything we receive is by the mercy of God.

We have learned a little bit about the life in Egypt, and we have completely abandoned the idea that there was slavery in the conventional sense. We understand that there was only slavery to the desire to receive for the self alone, to physical pleasure, and the people had no desire to leave. It is written, "because they were chased out of Egypt" (the portion of *Bo, the Book of Exodus*, chapter 12, verse 39), as if it is necessary to force inmates to be released from prison. Don't be mistaken; the Israelites had a very good life there. The idea that there was physical slavery has been a tremendous distraction from the true meaning of Passover.

Why is the month of *Nissan* controlled by the astrological sign of Aries and the planet Mars? Why is it called the month of freedom? And why do we need the fire signs? Mars is a fire planet and Aries is a fire sign. What is the significance of this?

When the ram was sacrificed, it was slaughtered to prevent it from dying in pain. And what did the Israelites do afterward? They burned it. People under the sign of Aries need to have the fire lit under their feet. Why and for what reason? This is the secret of life! When the ground is burning under our feet, we are not concerned with things such as "Did everyone see me? Does everyone know how important I am?" Instead we are dealing with pure survival, and in this situation we are all equal, without any ego. When the Israelites slaughtered and burned the ram, they removed the ego and corrected that aspect. This action is the key to true freedom.

In *Gate of Meditations*, the chapter on *Passover*, The Ari explains that the exile in the Diaspora is movement back from the state of manifestation to the state of potential. This is connected both to Passover and to the process of human aging. Why do we age? What is the phenomenon of old age? Science claims that every seven years, all the cells in our body are renewed. So if we are older than age seven, nothing remains in us physically from the body we were born with, and this process repeats every seven years. But after the age of 20, the process of renewal slows down and is delayed by various interfering factors. This, then, is the secret of aging: There is no aging process; there is only the effect of aging as a result of interference with the body's natural process of rejuvenation. Without this interference, we would remain young and healthy forever, and our physical bodies would never age beyond the age of seven.

Scientists don't understand the root of the interference that harms the rejuvenation mechanism, so they don't know how to restore the mechanism to proper functioning. They think that when the old cells are finished, new ones replace them. They don't understand that the cells are renewed every seven years. The Ari's explanation is about to cause a revolution in the scientific community. We will reveal the secret of the Fountain of Youth, because that is all that happens in Passover!

In *Gate of Meditations*, The Ari asks, "What is exile in the Diaspora?" He answers that it is first of all a return to the embryonic condition—to the potential state in which all the cells are undifferentiated. This is exactly the place or stage at which the interference with the rejuvenation mechanism takes place: The cells are prevented or delayed from returning to the undifferentiated, embryonic state. In the original process, each cell returns every seven years to its embryonic state, and its differentiated identity is erased. It goes through a form of cleansing and reconstruction as if it were in a special workshop, and when it emerges it is completely renewed, regaining its tissue identity.

The number of cells in our body does not grow after birth; during our lifetime, the only thing that takes place is renewal—the cells return to their embryonic state. So what interferes or prevents this process from occurring every seven years? The Ari answers that negative energy is to blame. A cancer cell is not different from any other cell, but negativity permeates it. It is "stuck" and cannot return to the embryonic state to be cleansed and renewed. The cure for cancer, and for any other sickness, is found in the holiday of Passover. The holiday lasts seven days, mirroring the lower seven emanations, and during these days we can be cleansed from negativity. We know that negativity attaches itself to the revelation of Light, which occurs in every cell with an individual tissue identity. The removal of the *Chametz* and the Passover sacrifices, together with the combinations— *Yud-Kaf-Shin* יכש, *Yud-Lamed-Yud* ילי, and *Chet-Bet-Vav* חבו —the *mikveh* and the consciousness of *The Zohar* remove the ego and the desire to receive for the self alone. In this way, negativity disappears from the cells, and in its absence we can continue the process of returning to the embryonic state—the reconstruction and cleansing. From there we can connect to the renewed revelation of the Light of *Zeir Anpin*, which was revealed during the Big Shabbat, and return to the state in which a healthy soul inhabits a healthy body.

Passover is spring, the renewal through which we can disconnect ourselves from all negativity. Passover is the time to open a new page in the book of our lives. That is exactly what Kabbalah teaches us—a new consciousness. From all of this, we come to understand that Passover is not connected only to tradition, and the *Seder* is not merely an elaborate family meal. We have no objection to pleasant family gatherings.

But we must not forget the true importance of this night: the historical event from 3,400 years ago, which has roots in Creation itself, and which literally recurs every year.

Rosh Chodesh Iyar
(TAURUS)

The month of *Iyar*, which falls under the astrological sign of Taurus, is the second month in the year.

It is important to remember that every new moon is an opportunity to connect to a force revealed in the universe through which we can attain control and order in our lives. This ability is not limited to only a few people; it is intended for every person in the world.

We can learn about the inner aspect of the month of *Iyar* in the portion of *Ki Tisa* in *The Zohar*. This is where all the troubles of the Israelites originated—the portion that deals with the Golden Calf.

In verse 21 it is written, "Said Rav Chiya: '... we see that the exile grows long, yet the son of David has still not come.'"

Rav Yosi responded that what enabled the Israelites to survive all the suffering of exile should be all the promises that the Creator had made. When they entered the synagogues and schools and learned of all the consolations presented in the holy books, their hearts were filled with happiness, and they could endure anything; without these consolations and promises, they could not have endured.

Any person who enters a synagogue in any of The Kabbalah Centres worldwide immediately sees the mercy that the Creator has for all the Israelites, and so he grows strong and certain that he will not be affected by all that is happening in the world. But *The Zohar* predicted that not every synagogue would reveal the knowledge of Kabbalah and the inner essence of the Torah. Instead, it was predicted that some would misinterpret verses from the text and conclude that it is not important to repent until the cup of sorrow is full. So it was inevitable that some generations would have difficulty enduring the suffering.

In the month of *Iyar*, there is a revelation of both destruction and healing. As it is written in the portion of *Beshalach*, after the 72 Names of God were given and after the splitting of the Red Sea had taken place, "I am God, your healer." On the other hand, in this month, during the Counting of the *Omer*, 24,000 students of Rav Akiva were killed. How, then, can we understand the significance of the month of *Iyar*?

Kabbalah explains that everything contains both a positive and a negative aspect, and we have the opportunity to choose which one we want to reveal. According to Abraham the Patriarch, as it is written in *The Book of Formation*, the Aramaic letters *Pei* פ and *Vav* ו are responsible for all the events that occur during this month. The letter *Pei* created the planet Venus, through which the universe receives the Light of the Creator in the month of *Iyar*. The letter *Vav* created the astrological sign of Taurus, which prescribes the way in which this Light will be revealed during the month. The Aramaic letters control the universe at the seed level. By studying Kabbalah and knowing the power of the Aramaic letters, we have the potential to gain control over the universe and destiny. From this we can conclude that we must study kabbalistic astrology in order to fulfill the true meaning of the verse "There is no luck to Israel."

A candle lights its surroundings in the same way regardless of whether it is surrounded by light or by darkness. We must behave in the same manner, spreading Light regardless of the behavior of those around us. If we wish to keep the connection to the Tree of Life, we must spread the Light as though it were a match and reveal unconditional love to everyone, regardless of the way they behave toward us. When the Israelites created the Golden Calf, they were governed by a desire to receive for the self alone. That is the reason they chose to use gold, which is connected to the left column and the desire to receive. But those who wish to stay connected to the Tree of Life must be concerned with the energy of sharing. This creates a connection to the spark of

Light within us, nourishing the soul with the abundance of the upper worlds. Whoever is busy sharing from a consciousness of Light will never feel any lack, just as a candle can light other candles without diminishing its flame.

In *The Zohar*'s discussion of *Ki Tisa*, Rav Yosi and Rav Abba agree that there is no need to wait for the Messiah, or to wait to "fill the cup of sorrow," because it is possible to repent at any moment. In other words, it is important that every person use the study of Kabbalah, *The Zohar*, and the 72 Names of God in order to change and restrict; this is the true meaning of repentance. *The Zohar* and these holy tools can open a window into the true world—a window through which we can share with others and receive the Light. The more we change and move forward in our spiritual work, the more the window will open, enabling us to share more and receive Light and blessings.

This is the key to coming out of bondage and bringing redemption to the world. The *Talmud* and *The Zohar* agree that the destruction of the Holy Temple and the subsequent exile were ultimately caused by hate for no reason and jealousy. In this condition, which the Israelites endured for the last 2,000 years, each person cares only for himself and assumes that no one else will ever care for him. Everyone knows that this way of living doesn't work. Although people think of themselves first, they still get old and die, and sorrow, suffering, and sickness persist throughout the world. The reason for this is simple: The window to the true world remains closed and locked. As long as the window is closed, there is no fulfillment of Light, and people experience want. But through repentance as described in *The Zohar*, we can bring redemption to the world, remove chaos, foster mind over matter, realize resurrection, and obtain immortality.

In *The Zohar*, it is written:

> After the death of the two sons of Aaron, Rav Yitzchak opened the discussion saying, "Serve Hashem in fear, and rejoice with trembling." It is also written, "Serve Hashem with gladness: come before Him with singing." These verses appear to contradict one another. But we have learned that to serve Hashem in fear means that one must first show fear and awe in every act he wishes to perform before his Master. As a result of this reverence before his Master, he will merit to serve with joy the commandments of the Torah. Therefore, it is written, "What does Hashem require of you but to fear? Through fear he will merit it all."

We must remember that the consciousness of every word in Aramiac is encoded in all the other words that can be written with the same letters. Another combination of letters that signifies the word fear יראה is the same letters as vision ראיה, to see. So we learn that fear of God is not only to be afraid but also to see Him. From seeing Him we can know Him, and in this way merit connecting with the Light. This interpretation is reinforced when Rav Abba quotes from the Torah: "The fear from Hashem is the genesis of knowledge."

To comprehend the inner consciousness of the month of *Iyar*, we read the verses that discuss the letters of the month in *The Book of Creation*: "He crowned the letter *Pei* and tied the crown around it and formed in it the planet Venus in the world and the fifth day in the year and the right nostril in the soul." And also, " He crowned the letter *Vav* and tied a crown around it and formed by it the bull in the world and the month of *Iyar* in the year and the left hand in the soul."

Let us now turn to the issue of healing. According to kabbalistic teachings, as expressed in the *Tikkun Hanefesh*, (see Diagram 6) the human body has more than the seven energy centers that are described in the Hindu chakra model. All the nations of the world received their knowledge from the same source: Abraham the Patriarch. As the Torah tells us, however, the children of Abraham's mistresses received presents, but Isaac, the son of Sarah, received everything Abraham possessed. We can infer from this that we received the entire knowledge from Abraham through Isaac the Patriarch, and the other nations received partial knowledge through the children of the mistresses who passed this knowledge on to the nations of the Far East.

Beginning in the year 5760 (2000), however, the entire world will discover the power of Kabbalah and the *Tikkun Hanefesh*. Everyone will use it as the foundation of medicine, and as a tool to eliminate any manifestation of chaos in the world. The *chakra* model is included in the *Tikkun Hanefesh*, so it cannot be the complete description of the energetic body. In the chakra model, for example, there is no specification of all the points in the head, a specification that is very significant.

It is important to emphasize the subject of *Tikkun Hanefesh* because *Iyar* is the month that reveals the power of spiritual healing, and the way to conduct this force is by using the *Tikkun Hanefesh*. A kabbalist practices the *Tikkun Hanefesh* five times a day to ensure the efficiency of the immune system and the spiritual protection against any aspect of chaos or sickness.

It is important to remember a principle emphasized by Rav Shimon in *The Zohar*: Knowledge is connection. The only way to connect to the healing power revealed in the universe is though the meditations attached to the *Tikkun Hanefesh*. Without these meditations, we can pray for healing from morning to night, but we will not achieve anything. Those who are connected to kabbalistic knowledge will see the days of the Messiah and the manifestation of the removal of death forever. In contrast, all the rest will be faced with judgment and the end of all existence.

Each letter in *The Book of Creation* carries cosmic information, just as radio waves serve as conduits for information in wireless communication networks. Abraham the Patriarch chose to call the second month by the name *Iyar* because he knew that 400 years into the future, it would be written so in the portion of *Beshalach*, in the verse "I am God your healer"—and this healing energy is passed to us though the letters *Pei* and *Vav*.

As simple as it sounds, this is the key to removing chaos from our lives. When we search for a solution to a problem or a cure for an illness, we are usually asked to trust complicated theories that only few scientists can understand. We are told that there is a high probability that the theories actually provide reasonable solutions to our problems. In the Age of Aquarius, however, this approach has reached the point of bankruptcy. Today, we demand to be given clear and convincing explanations for everything. We reject anything that is connected to probabilities, since probability means uncertainty, and uncertainty means chaos, sickness, and problems. Any probability model cannot channel the Light to remove sickness and solve the problems that interfere with our routines. With knowledge of Kabbalah, we will be able, in the month of *Iyar*, to inject the cosmos with healing energy in sufficient strength to remove chaos from the entire universe. The solution is not to be found in a laboratory. The solution exists throughout the universe, in the spiritual system that sustains us.

Lag B'Omer ~ DEATH ANNIVERSARY OF RAV SHIMON BAR YOHAI

The holiday known as *Lag B'Omer*, which falls on the 33rd day of the *Omer*, takes place during the month of Iyar, the second month of the year. It is completely under the influence of the *Counting of the Omer*. When Moses took the Israelites out of Egypt, they received freedom, liberty, and liberation without any effort on their part. For that reason, the Light of *Pesach* was withdrawn in order to give them (and us) the opportunity to work and earn all that Light that we received for free. This period of work is what is known as the *Counting of the Omer*. For 49 days—day after day—we have an opportunity to correct a different *Sfirah*. Seven weeks times seven days in each week equals 49. This connects us to the seven *Sfirot* of *Chesed* to *Malchut*.

Few people celebrate *Lag B'Omer* today, and even fewer understand its meaning. Throughout the generations until today, many atrocities have been connected to the days of the *Omer*: the destruction of both Holy Temples, the brutal massacre of 24,000 of Rav Akiva's students, and the start of the Holocaust. The *Talmud* discusses the massacre and explains that although the students were very elevated and knowledgeable in all aspects of the Torah, their deaths resulted from their lack of respect for one another. They were not capable of living with unity, love, and care. Rav Akiva's students did not know *The Zohar*. Kabbalah teaches that the Torah is a cosmic code and that *The Zohar* is the key that can be used to break the code. Without the key, there is no way to penetrate and receive from the Torah the message that is encoded within it. Years after these 24,000 deaths, Rav Shimon received *The Zohar* in a cave in Peki'in; he stated that 2,000 years later, a day would come when it would be possible to reveal to the public the real meaning of the biblical code.

The idea of *The Bible* as a moral code is an illusion. The Ten Commandments are not ten laws of human behavior. The concept that good people never lie or steal simply isn't real; it wasn't real even for most intelligent generations in the history of the nation of Israel—those present at the event on Mount Sinai. The knowledge available to that generation will not be revealed again until the time of the Messiah. But even with all their knowledge, these generations did not achieve the level of spirituality that would have merited entrance to the Land of Israel. Kabbalah teaches that the generation that will live in the time of Messiah—our present generation, according to Rav Abraham Azulai—is composed of the same souls that were present on Mount Sinai. They have been given a second chance to achieve the necessary spiritual level to bring the Messiah to the world.

When we discuss holidays, we are not dealing with religion; instead, we are concerned with the spiritual laws that form the basis on which the whole universe exists. This is not a philosophical or ethical system, but rather the base from which all physical reality has grown. Religion has never brought world peace, blessing, success, or health. The Ten Utterances have never prevented theft or killing. These changes will come only when the Light is felt in our lives. So when we discuss the holiday of *Lag B'Omer*, we must throw out all the religious explanations given to this day.

One reason given for this holiday—known to any traditional person—is that on this day the plague that had afflicted the students of Rav Akiva stopped. Verses 7—9 of chapter 25 in *the Book of Numbers* describe the plague that befell the Israelites in the desert, when Zimri son of Sola, the leader of the tribe of Shimon, committed adultery with a woman of Midian, Cozby. Then a man named Pinchas son of Eliezer son of Aaron The Cohen took a lance and stabbed Zimri and Cozby to death. With this action, the plague was stopped. But are we to believe that the plague stopped on *Lag B'Omer*. Kabbalah shows us a completely different picture, as well as a more realistic one. The connection to the inner meaning of *Lag B'Omer* is achieved by the *Counting of the Omer*.

But why do we count in that period, and why is it referred to as a time of judgment and negative energy? The Light that took the Israelites out of Egypt withdrew after the 15th day of the month of *Nissan*; on the 16th of *Nissan*, darkness returned to dwell all over the universe. Thus, during the 49 days after the Passover *Seder*, we have the opportunity to work spiritually in order to merit the Light of the Messiah that was revealed during the Exodus from Egypt. We must connect to the Light in a precise way, with the channel of communication tuned to the right frequency of Light at all times.

Every day there is a revelation of Light connected to a certain *Sfirah*, or emanation. The *Counting of the Omer* is a special form of software that enables us to connect to *Shavuot* as well as to the hardware of the Giving of the Torah. The *Counting of the Omer* was meant to save us from the pitfalls that are abundant during those 49 days by giving us the protocol for synchronized communication—the specific channel that enables us to enjoy continual satisfaction, even in a time of judgment, as a result of the affinity between the vessel and the Light's frequency, which changes every day. Every turn of the vessel from the Light's frequency prevents fulfillment and creates a state of uneasiness and hardship.

This is the technical explanation for the duality of this period, and it is a duality that also existed on the night of the Exodus. The Egyptians were hit by the plague of the firstborn, and the Israelites left strong. At the splitting of the Red Sea, the Israelites walked on dry land while all the Egyptians drowned. This is the duality of the universe. The same force, at the same time, can bring life or death, according to the vessel that is exposed to it. If you are wise, you build the right vessel in time and you merit life. During the *Counting of the Omer*, it is advisable to keep the gates closed in order to prevent any negative energy from entering. Every beginning creates an opening, and the time of the *Counting of the Omer* is so negative that there is a prohibition against marrying during this period—as well as against buying a new house or starting a new business.

On the 33rd day of the *Omer*, however, something completely different happens: A positive, intelligent energy that originates from the emanation of *Hod* is transmitted throughout the universe. It is similar to the energy of *Chesed* that made possible the splitting of the Red Sea. The judgment period of the *Omer* ends on *Lag B'Omer*.

Traditionalists say that Rav Shimon left this world on that day, which is why it became a holiday. But there are at least two reasons to contradict this explanation: First, the plague among the students of Rav Akiva stopped on that day many years before Rav Shimon died; and second, every event in the physical world is connected to the result and not to the cause. So we conclude that the plague stopped and that years later Rav Shimon chose to leave this world on the 33rd day of the *Omer* because of the special energy characteristic to that day, not the other way around. It is important to understand that no occurrence in the physical world creates a holiday. Material events are always results, and holidays are connected to the realm or cause—to cosmic events in the spiritual realm of reality. The fruit is always included in the seed. Rav Shimon chose to leave this world on *Lag B'Omer* because of the cosmic energy that characterizes this day every year. On this day, a huge Light is turned on in the universe that removes all the darkness. That is the reason the plague stopped on this day.

Thought creates reality. Modern physics has adopted this way of thinking but hasn't found a way to use that knowledge to control matter completely. Today, in the age of computers, instead of strengthening the power of thought, many people relinquish the use of this powerful tool in their head and are content with basic functioning on the robotic level, with no free choice. Only thought determines who we are and what we will achieve in life. *Lag B'Omer* is a holiday because on that day, the cosmic thought energy achieves the peak of perfection in the seed level. The plague that killed Rav Akiva's students stopped because the volume of the Light overcame the negativity created by the hatred that existed between the students.

At the end of the *Counting of the Omer*, *Shavuot* is revealed in the material realm. As a result of *Lag B'Omer*, we can connect to *Shavuot* much more easily. In a sense, *Lag*

B'Omer is inseparable from *Shavuot*. All the Light of *Shavuot* is revealed, but we need to elevate to an alternative awareness—a kind of soul elevation—in order to connect to that Light. We are connecting to the energy that the Creator shares with us in order to benefit His creation. And we make the connection by using the meditations written by the kabbalists. However, it is not enough to pray with a *Siddur* (prayer book) that has all the meditations; it is also necessary to know and understand what we are connecting to. If we read and study and pray without knowing the reason, then we haven't created any connection to the energy transmitted in the universe. On the night of *Lag B'Omer*, we connect to the original energy of *Shavuot*, which is a higher level than that available on the holiday of *Shavuot* itself.

To create this connection, we read *The Zohar* portion called "the small assembly," or *Ha Idra Zuta Kadisha*.

After Rav Shimon and Rav Elazar came out of the cave in Peki'in, they gathered eight students in a cave on the way between Tsefat and Meron. There Rav Shimon revealed for the first time the secrets of *The Zohar*. This group of ten people is called "the big assembly," or Ha Idra Rabba, in *The Zohar*. Rav Shimon was a reincarnation of Moses, and he received *The Zohar* by connecting to the roots of his soul: Moses and Elijah the prophet. During the study of *The Zohar* in the *Idra Rabba*, tremendous Light was revealed that caused two of the students to finish their correction and leave this world in a very special way (described in *The Zohar*). The smaller group that remained, consisting of eight people, was then called the *Idra Zuta*, and with them Rav Shimon continued the teaching of *The Zohar*.

On *Lag B'Omer*, Rav Shimon summoned Light to be revealed in the world, and in this way he was able to stop the plague among 24,000 of Rav Akiva's students. Years later, on exactly the same day, he chose to leave the world. On that day he invited his six students to a final lesson described in the "small assembly" section of *The Zohar*. As it is written, "And we learned in that day that Rav Shimon wanted to leave this world and was arranging his things, all the friends gathered at Rav Shimon." In *The Gate of the Holy Spirit*, Rav Isaac Luria explains that the day a righteous person leaves this world is a happy occasion. On that day, the righteous person is able to erase completely the negative energy connected with his body, and all the positive energy the righteous person has manifested throughout his life is gathered and revealed.

Nowhere else in The Bible is there a story about someone choosing the day of their death. Even though he was not on the level of the patriarchs and was not a chariot to any emanation, Rav Shimon merited choosing the day of his death. But why did he choose this day, when the nation of Israel needed him most? Why didn't he die on the following day? Rav Shimon knew ahead of time that he had to leave this world while he was still in perfect health. Rav Shimon did not want to retire from this world, but he found out that he had to do it. Why? *The Zohar* reveals that the snake—the Angel of Death, the personification of the negative intelligent energy—came before the Creator with a highly unusual complaint. At the time of the first restriction, the snake was created to give people free will, the ability to choose between desire for the self alone or desire to receive in order to share. "For that reason," said the snake, "I exist. I can convince people in many different ways that they should steal, lie, or kill. That is my job from the beginning of time. But lately something exceptional has happened: Rav Shimon is chasing me. All the people run away from me except Rav Shimon. He chases me and makes me run away from him. To tell you the truth, I haven't found one place in the world where I can hide from him. Therefore, Creator, if you don't ask Rav Shimon to leave this world, I will be forced to do it myself, and mankind will lose its free will before they merit the Messiah, before they finish their correction, and before they remove the Bread of Shame that preceded the restriction and the whole Creation." The Creator then turned to Rav Shimon and told him, "The revelation of Light you brought to the world completely removed the negative element from the universe and caused the removal of free will from the people. Therefore, you must leave this world." Since Rav Shimon had to leave, he chose to do so on *Lag B'Omer*.

During that night, the revelation of the Light reaches a peak and is transmitted throughout the universe. *Lag B'Omer* is parallel to *Shavuot*, the Giving of the Torah, but on a higher level, because in *Shavuot* the external aspect of the Torah is revealed in the material world, whereas in *Lag B'Omer* we receive the inner aspect of the Torah and its soul.

We receive the entire potential in the spiritual world within the Torah. Rav Shimon chose to leave this world on this day in order to help us connect to this high energy. The Torah doesn't reveal to us the meaning of *Lag B'Omer*; Rav Shimon decided to give us this essential information. Rav Shimon chose to enlist this day's complete spiritual force—a task that he could achieve only on the day of his death.

After the death of any person, the body is buried in the ground because its consciousness is similar to that of the ground: the desire to receive for the self alone. When the body decays and deteriorates, it is unifying with the dirt around it; the material process expresses the spiritual one. In a righteous person, however, body consciousness has been transformed. A righteous person is someone who successfully controls body consciousness with soul consciousness—someone who manages to completely neutralize the body's desire to receive for the self alone. There is no more reason to combine it with the dirt. The body already reached the level of the soul, and therefore it does not go through the process of decay and deterioration that occurs in the body of any other deceased person. In most people, the soul feeds the body and keeps it alive, but in the righteous person it is the other way around: The body becomes the slave of the soul; the body cancels its consciousness and is busy servicing the soul.

According to *The Zohar*, when a righteous person's body is buried, it remains intact as in his life; it never decays in the grave. Every year, on the anniversary of their death, all righteous people visit their own gravesites, reconnect to their bodies, and reveal their Light, just as it was revealed on the day of their death. Righteous people preserve their bodies in the graves to make it easier for us to connect to them. If we connect to a righteous person on his death anniversary, we can gain some of his strength and remove negativity from our lives. The extent to which we will be successful in removing negativity depends on the extent of our connection to the Light. *Lag B'Omer*, with the help of Rav Shimon and with the knowledge of all that was mentioned here, helps us connect to a stronger force than that revealed on *Shavuot*.

So as we learn from Rav Luria and Rav Shimon, *Lag B'Omer* is a day of happiness. This day gives us an excellent opportunity for a correction of *karet* by studying *The Zohar* all night. What is *karet*, and what is its origin? *karet* (amputated) means separation from the Light. Every sin and every negative action we commit, be it premeditated or by accident, separates us a little from the Light. Rav Isaac Luria teaches us that we can repair and reconnect the communication channels by studying the Torah and *The Zohar* every night. This action of correction is the same as the repentance we do during the month of *Tishrei*: We go back in time to the negative event and correct what needs to be fixed at its root. A correction of *karet* is more effective when done at a time when the energy is especially positive than when it is performed on a night when we lack cosmic support. Furthermore, a correction of *karet* done with a group of people who all meditate on the same thing is even more effective than an individual act. Rav Shimon suggests doing the correction on the night of *Lag B'Omer*, because on this night the *Counting of the Omer* ends in the upper world. The complete spiritual potential embodied in the Torah is revealed at this time, and this is a huge revelation of Light.

The result of *Lag B'Omer* becomes apparent in the material world after two weeks, at *Shavuot*. At that time it is possible to spiritually "see" from one end of the world to the other, with no interruptions. We can understand and see the future, and there is no higher blessing than that. But we live each day in the physical world, not in the endless spiritual world. And for that reason, Rav Shimon built for us a living bridge. Rav Shimon himself is the bridge, because like Moses, he grabs hold of the Tree of Life and the Endless on the one hand, and on the other hand his physical body is buried in our world. Since he chose to leave the world on *Lag B'Omer*, Rav Shimon can connect to his body on this day and thereby become a living bridge for us. With this living bridge, we can elevate our consciousness up to the cosmic level of *Binah*, just as we can during the month of *Tishrei*. This elevation creates a foundation in us for the power of "removal of death," which gives us "life insurance" from *Shavuot* to Rosh Hashanah.

At *Lag B'Omer*, in addition to mentioning all the qualities of the righteous, we follow the path laid down for us by Rav Shimon and study *The Zohar* itself, which is the best tool for spiritual connection.

Another tradition in *Lag B'Omer* is the first haircut for boys, which takes place when they are three years old. What is the origin of this tradition? During the first three years of life, a child's skull changes and grows because it consists of a several bones with a small membrane in between. At the end of the third year, the membrane is finally closed and the skull becomes hardened. This physical process expresses a spiritual change in the child. From birth until the age of three, the child is exposed to raw spiritual energy emanating from the upper worlds. In order to draw this raw spiritual energy, the child uses his hair as an antenna, which channels the energy to the right place while insulating it on the way. This age is characterized by what adults call a "fertile imagination"—a completely different perception of reality. Often adults cannot comprehend a child's logic, but our sages teach that since the destruction of The Temple, the power of prophecy has been given to fools and children. In both groups, the curtain between man and the spiritual world is partly torn, giving them access to knowledge that is hidden from the rest of us.

At the age of three, the child loses his uninterrupted connection to the source of raw energy. Why do we cut the child's hair on *Lag B'Omer*? On that day, especially with the help of Rav Shimon, the child is able to reconnect to the source of raw energy, but this time the energy is changed into controlled energy. Closing the curtain over the spiritual energy in the head is done in order to reveal the potential that exists in that energy.

The Zohar describes what happened to Rav Shimon in the upper worlds. The Creator wanted to destroy the world and sent the Angel of Death on that mission. When the Angel of Death descended to the world, Rav Shimon came to meet him and sent him back to the Creator with a contradictory message: The world must not be destroyed if 30 righteous people can be found. Rav Shimon made certain that the Angel of Death informed the Creator that he didn't complete his mission because Rav Shimon made a different decree. Some time later, the Angel of Death returned to the world. Again Rav Shimon blocked his way and said, "Didn't I tell you to return to the upper world and never to return? If you are back because 30 righteous persons are not enough to save the world, then I demand that you return to the Creator and tell him that I, Rav Shimon, am in the world, and that is enough to sustain the entire world and prevent you from destroying it!"

Indeed, the Angel of Death returned to the Creator, gave him the message from Rav Shimon, and never returned. It is true that negative things can happen in the world as a result of people's negative actions, but the righteous can cancel them. Only Rav Shimon was capable of channeling the happy life energy to the world in sufficient volume to cancel the plague. And that is why only he merited connection with *Lag B'Omer*—the day of the tremendous Light of the inner Torah in our world, a day of cosmic happiness—in his death as in his life.

The purpose of Kabbalah is not only to transfer information, but also to open the cosmic channels necessary to ensure our spiritual and physical well-being so that we may fulfill the purpose of our existence. All the power of science has not brought unity between people, although they were meant be unified. It may seem that a separated and fragmented world is the ruling state. But this is an illusion, and in order to destroy the illusion on this powerful day on our cosmic calendar, Rav Shimon again brought the human race to the Revelation Event.

Rosh Chodesh Sivan
(GEMINI)

One of the most difficult problems for anyone who learns or teaches Kabbalah is the phenomenon of people who revolt against the cosmic law according to which the world was created. Even if they recognize what a mistake they're making, people will refuse to break old habits and to develop new and more positive ones. They can even recognize that change is possible and beneficial but still refuse to implement it.

We can look at periods of our lives as a chain of islands connected by paved bridges. After each change comes a period of temporary stability, like an island that gives a sense of calm—but only until the next change, of course. We are used to this pattern, and we tend to believe that life must be this way. It seems to us that we have no control over the intermittent chaos that directs our lives in an unpredictable path.

In the month of *Sivan* (Gemini) we have the holiday of *Shavuot*. In order to understand the meaning of this holiday and this month, we will first read from *The Zohar* and then return to reveal the unique energy of the month of *Sivan*.

As quoted by The Ari, *The Zohar* states, "And you should know that whoever doesn't sleep in this night (the night of *Shavuot*) at all, not even for a moment, and deals with the Torah all night, is insured to complete his year and no harm will fall on him during this year."

This is an amazing passage. What it means is that if we are careful and stay awake the whole time to make a spiritual connection on the night of *Shavuot*, we are assured that we will not be forced to leave this world at least until the end of the current year. On the night of *Shavuot*, we can connect to the power of "removal of death" on a level that is sufficient for four months. Four months without chaos! Nothing in the world, with the exception of knowledge of Kabbalah, can supply us with such a treasure.

To better understand the connection between the month of *Sivan* and the holiday of *Shavuot*, we need to go back for a moment to the night of *Hoshanah Rabba*, which "seals" the holiday of *Sukkot*. After midnight, we can go out to check the shadow by the light of the moon. With this check, we can determine whether we have enough life energy to sustain us for a whole year.

The light of the moon on that night is different from any other source of light at any other time. The shadow we check is different from any other shadow we have at any other time in life. It is a spiritual shadow that indicates the density of the life energy in every area of our body. Like an x-ray, this special shadow reveals inner flaws in our body—but unlike an x-ray, the shadow also reveals the future. This shadow has a special name: *Tselem* (*Tsel* צֵל in Aramaic is shadow; *Tselem* refers to an image, specifically "in God's image"). From the Book of Genesis, we learn that *Tselem* צֶלֶם is also a mold, an image. Men were created in the mold and image of the Creator, as a copy true to the original.

The *Tselem* actually represents a consciousness rather than any physical form. The *Tselem*'s consciousness is that of unity and harmony. This same consciousness exists among all the physiological and psychological activities in the body at any given moment. If a person hurts his finger, the whole body immediately unites in the task of repairing and healing the wound. The attention, the position of the body, the level of activity, the blood pressure and pulse, the breathing rhythm, the metabolic rate, the oxygen supply at the site of the wound—all these indicate that every cell in the body is affected by the event and is drafted to the war effort. One for all, and all for one!

According to the *Tselem* consciousness, we can understand that all the people in the world are united at the spiritual level, which science calls the quantum level; we were all created in the image of God. All people have a similar mission at this level: to reveal the Light throughout the universe. All mankind are responsible for one another, and need each other to achieve the final correction and the redemption of the world. The consciousness of the *Tselem* focuses the personal identity and the personal interest on one common need. No cell in the body rests until the wound has formed a cast. The personal identity of each cell receives a positive meaning: Every cell has talents that can help achieve the general mission. This consciousness of complete unity duplicates the Light, because only in the Light is there no separation.

According to *The Ari*, the message and consciousness of the astrological sign of Gemini in general, and the holiday of *Shavuot* specifically, concentrates in one point: *Tselem*. The *Tselem* consciousness is even higher than the consciousness of immortality. This is a force that can harmonize and unify everything in the universe, at any level or aspect. Recognizing this force and including it in our daily activities can revolutionize the quality of life all over the world. Such an improvement and a change of our destiny for the better are the goals that Kabbalah sets for us.

To some extent, achieving these goals is a matter of acquiring knowledge, but this intellectual aspect is secondary. It is only the first step on our path to the goal: the manifestation of ideas and the achievement of control over our destiny in a way that will enable us to finish our correction—and complete the purpose of the entire Creation in full cooperation with the Creator. For we wish to improve not only our own destiny, but also that of the entire civilization. We strive to control the destiny of the entire universe. A complete spiritual and physical manifestation of the "unified field theory" to the level of complete unification with the Creator—this is the meaning of the Force of the *Tselem*. Religion says, Pray to the Creator in times of hardship. The *Tselem* says, You are the Creator. The force of the Creator is within you. Let it flow through you, and the miracle will immediately take place.

Tselem is the life force that beats within all of us, that gives us life and sustains it. Our intelligence confuses us into thinking that each of us is essentially different and separated from the other. This is an illusion fed to us by the Opponent. The purpose of studying Kabbalah is to bring us back to the origin of Creation and to connect us to the force of the *Tselem* acting within us and sustaining us. The path there contradicts logic: Believe, and then you will see. There is no logical way to explain how, although the entire reality points to a wide array of different and weird creations—inanimate, plant, living and speaking. Despite all these, the physicists arrived at the idea of the "unified field theory"—an idea that apparently contradicts all the findings in the physical world.

In the Torah it is written, at the end of the portion of *Bamidbar*, that in order for the Levis working in the Temple not to die, they had to comply with one specific rule. The common expression of this rule is that it was forbidden to look at the Ark of the Covenant with the naked eye, and whoever disobeyed this rule would die from the force of the Light. Thus, there was an instruction that the Ark must always be covered. Yet the Torah uses the phrase "to swallow" rather than "to look" or "to see." It is as if someone would try to eat the Ark. It is true that if I swallow water or food, the moment they enter my body no one will be able to see them. But why use such an indirect expression to convey such a simple idea? There is an essential difference between something that disappears inside me after I swallow it and something I covered with a mask or a handkerchief. A mask or a handkerchief still makes it possible to see the shape of the thing. By contrast, something that is swallowed disappears and cannot be identified—neither its shape nor even its existence. The lesson the Torah is conveying is very special: When the Levis covered the Ark, the Ark simply disappeared, as if by magic. The covering was visible, but it was impossible to recognize the shape of the thing it was concealing. Why? Because the Ark of the Covenant lost its separate identity, and only its *Tselem* remained.

After being covered, the Ark spread out from 1% consciousness to 99% consciousness. The Ark actually returned to its embryonic state, just as an embryo's cells cannot be identified at the beginning of pregnancy, and we cannot say which cell will develop into a heart and which will be the liver. The cells actually exist, but their essence is unseen. We can learn an important lesson from this: The unified cells develop into classified tissues, but the tissues never lose the unified aspect from which they developed.

The *Tselem* is everywhere and everything. All the cells of the body are 99% similar. That is the truth. The specification is nothing more that an illusory effect. Who told a certain cell in the embryo to develop into an eye and another to become an ear? There must be a spiritual aspect beyond the physical one that established the reality. This is the *Tselem Elokim*. When we truly love people, we identify with them as ourselves. We feel their feelings as if they were ours. This is the unity of the *Tselem*.

Separation from the *Tselem* is what prevents us from creating miracles and revealing the complete Light force of the Creator in the world. This is what *The Ari* teaches us. In the night of *Hoshanah Rabba*, the moon shines on us the force of the *Tselem* and rules our physical body with it. With the help of the astrological sign of Gemini and the holiday of *Shavuot*, we can reprogram our consciousness and exchange the analytical, illusory consciousness for the real *Tselem* consciousness. In this way, spirit will rule matter, and we will materialize the Light within us and achieve control over the destiny of the universe.

If in the body there is a sickness or a certain deficiency, the *Tselem* can heal it. The closest thing to a physical expression of the *Tselem* is the DNA in the nuclei of cells. Since DNA duplicates the cells in a manner that enables any wound to heal and all the cells to be replaced every seven years, why can't it tell the body of an amputee to grow a new leg? Physiologically it is possible; the physical infrastructure exists. Only doubt and negative consciousness prevent these kinds of miracles from happening every day.

Biologically, an amputated arm can grow again just like a nail or hair. Until the age of seven, all the atoms in the body of a child are renewed. The body we are using at this moment is not the same physical body with which we were born, and not even the same body we used ten years ago. Doctors know this but keep it a secret, just as the kabbalists kept their knowledge a secret. Actually, this knowledge is documented in medical journals and is announced in professional seminars, but no one knows what to do with it, or how to use it for the benefit of the people of the world.

How is it that all the cells of the body unite in a split second to help heal a small cut in the finger, and millions of biochemical actions take place to heal the wound? If you remember this question, you have received 99% of the ability to connect with your inner essence. There must be a divine essence within us that causes this. Once we understand this basic fact, we will start to enable the *Tselem* to influence all aspects of our daily life. And the month of *Sivan* gives us the best opportunity to cultivate this understanding.

The astrological sign of this month is Gemini. Gemini is the clue to the energy that controls this month throughout the universe. Gemini—which is signified by twins, like the two angels on the Ark—represents two aspects of one thing and expresses the unity of the differences, the consciousness of the *Tselem*. The only reason we treat people as separate individuals is the illusory consciousness controlled by the negative side.

When a friend or a family member is in trouble, we rush to his help—not as a stranger, but as part of us. We make an effort for him, just as we would do for ourselves if we were in his place. In the same manner, we must approach the idea of "soul mates." These are not merely two people acting in harmony but, as *The Ari* describes in *The Gate of Reincarnation*, are actually two parts of one soul that found their way to one another. One soul was separated into a male part and a female part, and these parts were reincarnated as a boy baby and a girl baby that came to this world. When they matured, they found each other and reunited in the form of marriage. In the same way, we can say that the cut finger was separated from the head and the heart and the liver during the development of the embryo in the womb. Yet in their essence, they are still one. The *Tselem* consciousness makes it possible for us to rise above the illusion of separation.

With the aid of this attitude, there is no need to turn to the Creator for help; we can just unite with the Creator. When we become the Creator, we can create any miracle we need. But once we achieve this level, what else is left for us to do in the world of the living? There is only one more test to pass: the test of certainty. Every day Satan will test us with different tests; he will confront us with predicted and unpredictable challenges; he will provide us with reasons to get mad, to give up, to see the separation. Or we can continue to rise above all the illusions, continue trusting the Light to be united with the Creator, and create solutions to all those illusory problems. We can command the car to start and drive, just as we would expect God to do. We can split the Red Sea. Kabbalah teaches that it wasn't God who split the Red Sea. The people did it, using the right consciousness, with the 72 Names of God and with the Light they channeled into the world. The *Tselem* is capable of coordinating million of activities in the body because it is in certainty with regard to the Light.

Our test is to be in unity with the unpleasant neighbor, with the IRS clerk, with the bank manager who made our check bounce, with the strict and inconsiderate boss. Only the one who is capable of overcoming all these tests has the merit to see the revelation of Light everywhere and at all times in his life.

If the car doesn't start, it doesn't mean that Kabbalah doesn't work, but rather that we didn't connect to the Light at the certainty level necessary, and therefore we were not capable of starting the car. We can command a sickness to leave our body because it is our territory. The level of our success depends on our level of certainty in the Light. The sixth of *Sivan*, *Shavuot*, gives us the opportunity to connect with the consciousness of certainty and unity that is needed to reveal all layers of reality. The Torah does this as well. The Torah is only the clothing, the illusion, of God's message. Only by learning and implementing Kabbalah in our daily life can we connect to the Light and reveal the true and complete reality.

On Mount Sinai, all the nations received the Torah and the Ten Utterances, but every nation received it in their language. Only the Israelites received the Torah in Aramaic, with the help of the letters of the month, *Reish* ר and *Zain* ז —channels of communication that connect us to the Light that exists in the inner Torah. The other nations of the world received the weaker message, through the veils of the illusory world, understood in different languages.

This is the reason they were separated from the Light, and therefore were not asked to take upon themselves severe conditions for their survival during the revelation. The nations of the world were safe from any excess Light by the usual veils of earthly consciousness, a limited and final desire, and a language other than Hebrew. The message is simple: The secret of life is the connection with the Light. The secret of success in the world lies in the ability to connect to the Light force of the Creator and channel it through us. Only in a month with this consciousness can the Torah be revealed.

Shavuot

The true meaning of the holiday of *Shavuot* has been lost and forgotten. During the holidays in the month of *Tishrei*, we see people visiting the synagogues, but *Shavuot* is a forgotten holiday. No one remembers, or understands today, the reason for the Creator's presentation of the Torah on Mount Sinai 3,400 years ago.

We must struggle with the indisputable fact that people accept the way of life that has been dictated to them. We notice that there is a predetermined chain of events—one that we find very hard to change. Unexpected changes often occur around us. We move from one firm state to another, connected by periods of instability. We enter a new state when the previous one ends. These changes take place regardless of our intentions, and we have no say in them. We accept the changes and accept the fact that they are necessary. There are certain changes in life that we expect, such as a *Bar* or *Bat Mitzvah* (when a boy reaches the age of 13 and a girl reaches the age 12), both of which occur at a known time; sometimes they are accompanied by biological or mental changes, but they do not necessarily indicate in a change in the person himself. Can we recognize a change in the person? Do these events mean anything to us? Can they be changed? These are the questions no one asks. Our difficulty lies in taking a more active role in shaping our lives.

We learn from *The Zohar* that every night of *Shavuot*, Rav Shimon and his students stayed awake and studied Torah. In Israel, *Shavuot* is celebrated only one day. Outside of Israel, it is observed for two days. But what exactly is observed? According to the rule we learned from Rav Brandwein (my teacher), the fact that many ignore this event is proof of its importance. If it were not so important, the negative side would not bother to remove people's attention from it.

People have disconnected from the importance of the event on Mount Sinai because it is considered part of a religious tradition. And tradition has only one purpose: to commemorate an event from the past. Yet no one sees the point in commemorating an event that occurred 3,400 years ago as long as they cannot perceive the direct and immediate connection between that event and our life today. For that reason, Rav Shimon—and, 1,500 years after him, The Ari— explain the meaning of this holiday in modern terms. Rav Shimon says, in effect, that every year on *Shavuot* we can purchase life insurance. Nothing can afflict the insured. No human insurance company can give such service to its customers! But had Rav Shimon not stated this clearly (introduction to *The Zohar*, volume 1, page 148, verse 150), no one would believe that such a thing is possible. Whoever makes the right spiritual connection on *Shavuot* has been insured—they will not die or be hurt at least until the following *Rosh Hashanah*. In a world where people don't know what will happen tomorrow, there is no price for the type of insurance Rav Shimon is offering us. From this we can understand that the reason to celebrate *Shavuot* is not religious or historical tradition, but rather pure self-interest.

The Ari quotes *The Zohar* as follows: "And know that all those who don't sleep in this night (the night of *Shavuot*) at all, not even for one minute, and study Torah all night, are promised to complete the year and they will suffer no harm that year." This incredible portion of *The Zohar* tells us that if we follow this strict instruction regarding the spiritual connection on the night of *Shavuot*, we are promised that nothing will harm us and we will not have to leave this world, at least until the end of that year. On the night of *Shavuot* we can connect to the force of "removal of death" to a sufficient extent to last four months. Four months without chaos! Nothing in this world, except the knowledge of Kabbalah, can provide such a return!

But what exactly happened on Mount Sinai 3,400 years ago? What is the secret of this wonderful event? On Mount Sinai, all the nations of the world received the Torah and the

Ten Utterances. We learn from the *Midrash* that before the Torah was given to the Israelites, The Creator offered it to all the nations of the world—and all refused to accept it. The commentators explain that The Creator offered it first to the other nations because a day will come when all the nations will regret the fact that they refused to accept the Torah. And when this day comes, they will turn to The Creator and ask, "Why didn't you give us the Torah?" And to that The Creator will give them the answer He prepared 3,400 years ago: "I turned to you first, but you refused my offer." According to tradition, when the Creator turned to the Israelites, they answered, "We will do and we will hear." But the *Talmud* describes the event in a different and less ideal way. According to the *Talmud*, The Creator gave the Israelites an ultimatum. He elevated Mount Sinai in the air, collected the Israelites in the crater that lay underneath, and said to them, "Either accept the Torah or this will be your burial ground." Under these circumstances, the Israelites said what anyone would have said: "We will do, and we will hear." But today, as was the case then, most people are not excited about the Torah. So what is the point of *Shavuot*?

Why was the Torah given on that specific day? It is not coincidence. *Shavuot* is the only day of the year that is perfect for this mission. *The Zohar* reveals that timing has a decisive meaning in our world. Timing determines if a person will be rich or poor, sick or healthy, patient or intolerant. An action in a positive time will bring success, even if a stupid person does it. With negative timing, even a genius is destined to fail sooner or later. On the holiday of *Shavuot* and in the event of the giving of the Torah, the Creator gave us a very special opportunity that necessitated very specific energetic prerequisites—prerequisites that occur only on the sixth day of the month of *Sivan*.

Only during the month governed by this energy could the Torah be revealed. Every month the Light of the Creator embodied in the Torah is revealed in the world, but the revelation is channeled through negative aspects of separation and differentiation. During any other month, we would have looked at the Ten Utterances as laws—ten commands dictating that you shall not steal, you shall not kill, and so forth. Only in the month of *Sivan* can we grasp the keys to elevate our consciousness with inner truth. You will not hurt another, not because it is the law but because the other is a part of you. The Ten Utterances don't describe a perfect social order or some kind of utopia, but rather the result of being in the right consciousness. By connecting to the Light, there will be no need for judge or legislator or policeman to make us follow laws imposed on us from without.

On *Shavuot*, we can connect to immortality. *The Zohar* says that on Mount Sinai, during the event of the giving of the Torah, there was "removal of death." At that event the correction was finished, and freedom from the Angel of Death was achieved: freedom from chaos, and freedom from any manifestation of Satan consciousness in the world. This freedom was a result of the illumination of the entire world with the Light of the Creator, a Light of life and perfection. This illumination enabled each person to see beyond time and space, from one end of the world to the other, and to achieve complete control and certainty regarding all aspects of his life, including future events. The revelation of *Shavuot* included not only the Ten Utterances but also the enormous life energy in such a scale as to cancel completely the consciousness of death. And since there is no lack in the spiritual realm, energy does not disappear; what happened once on Mount Sinai must happen again every year in the entire universe on the sixth day of *Sivan*.

By taking the advice of Rav Shimon and The Ari, we can connect with this huge life energy. But there is a very specific way to establish this connection: We must draw the Light while practicing restriction. The Ten Utterances teach us how to practice restriction in our lives. Whoever is exposed to the enormous Light of *Shavuot* without a proper spiritual vessel will be burned; that was the message the Creator conveyed to the people when he coerced them into accepting the Torah. When that awesome Light is revealed in the world, either you connect to it through the consciousness explained in the Torah and gain eternal life and the end of the correction process, or the huge Light will burn you. This is not a punishment but rather a physical result of lack of compatibility between the vessel and the Light—just as an appliance built to conduct 110 volts of electricity will burn when it is fed 220 volts, without discounts, reductions, or exceptions.

During the Exodus from Egypt, the Israelite nation was only a potential. When the Israelites said, "We will do," they created a new situation. On the individual level, the spiritual vessels were made compatible by revealing and connecting to the Ten Utterances—by learning the way to practice restriction. But this concept was also established on the cosmic level. On the sixth day of *Sivan*, the whole universe is able to receive the energy of the sun without being burned. During the giving of the Torah on Mount Sinai, we were protected by the cosmic energy from the abundance of Light revealed by the Creator in the world.

The Israelites became the channels for this awesome Light force only in order to provide a "community service" to the universe. According to *The Zohar*, the Israelites are supposed to channel the Light of the Creator and pass it to all humankind. If there is sickness in the world, if there is war, if the paint is chipping in any building around the world, it is only for one reason: The Israelite didn't do his/her job of transferring enough Light to the world.

In order to successfully complete their mission, the Israelites received tools: a central antenna to collect Light, and intelligent channels of communication to spread that Light. The antenna is the Land of Israel, and the channels of communication are the letters of the Aramaic alphabet. There is no other reason to use the Aramaic language or to have the Israelites live in Israel. It is not because of the merit of the fathers, but the duty of the sons in every generation. It is not a territory but rather a tool for spiritual connections. Whoever is not connected to the spiritual essence of Israel—whoever does not make the spiritual connections for the whole world at every prayer—goes into the synagogue empty and comes out an empty vessel. Rav Shimon Bar Yochai, who was certainly not an anti-Semite or an anti-Israelite, said this 2,000 years ago. A spiritual connection to Israel makes it possible for us to draw spiritual abundance to the world even if we are physically living in a different country.

At the Revelation Event, we didn't receive ten commands, but rather ten levels of Light, health, love, continuity and security. But at that moment we couldn't contain the Light and reveal it in our everyday lives. The Light was in potential. At the Revelation, it can be said that we received an electrical battery. After 40 days, Moses descended holding a Light bulb in his hands—an object that can reveal the potential in the battery. The Torah and the stone tablets are the physical appliances with which to reveal the Light of the Creator in the world.

When the Israelites built the Golden Calf, they assumed that Moses would be the intermediary between them and the Light. They were not searching for a replacement for God, as we are often told, but rather a replacement for the Torah: a different spiritual appliance to contain and reveal the potential Light received on *Shavuot*. The Light revealed on Mount Sinai is the same Light that will be revealed in the time of the Messiah in the Age of Aquarius. We must learn to optimize this energy and take care of it, or it might cause a huge disaster, God forbid, that may affect all of us.

By using the right tools, we can achieve a balanced flow of abundance. By studying the Torah and *The Zohar* throughout the night of *Shavuot*, we connect to the channel that draws for us, in a controlled way, the spiritual plenitude revealed on Mount Sinai, in exactly the same manner as the first Torah scroll that Moses received in those 40 days on Mount Sinai. We are nourished by a life force that removes chaos and the Angel of Death from our midst, at least until the end of the year.

This is what Rav Shimon teaches us. Unfortunately, the Israelites didn't wait for Moses and lost the opportunity to finish the entire correction of humankind. Every year at *Shavuot*, however, we get a chance to correct part of that historical mistake. Rav Shimon suggests that we "keep busy" with the Torah all that night. Conventional religion teaches that we should stay awake on *Shavuot* because the Israelites went to sleep that night, and we don't want to repeat their mistakes. Do you find this convincing? It is a negative statement—one that tells us not to repeat a mistake. Being busy with the Torah really means investing the same effort a person puts into his career or his business, where he toils from morning until night. Beyond that, just as we look at a business as a practical and useful undertaking, so should we look at the Torah. We must use the Torah and put it to use in our daily lives. But how is it possible to use the Torah? Only together with the wisdom of Kabbalah.. Otherwise the Torah is merely a book that only a select few are willing to study. People can't connect with the Torah as long as they don't practice Kabbalah in their lives. Only Kabbalah teaches that there is a positive and practical reason for study, which is to inject Light into the entire world and into ourselves by using the power of the Aramaic letters and the communication system of Kabbalah.

The combinations of Aramaic letters used to write the Ten Utterances is a communication channel that transmits the removal of death and the Light of the Creator. This is the secret of the Ten Utterances; the content of the text is secondary in importance. If a person wants to reconnect to his spiritual self, he automatically understands "thou shalt not kill" because he would never do that to himself. You can take someone else's life only if you exist in separation. For this reason, the command is secondary. It was never the real purpose.

Four hundred years ago, Rav Abraham Azulai said that the decree of prohibition had been lifted, and it was possible to study Kabbalah freely. This means that the level of restriction in the world had changed. If until 400 years ago it was possible to reveal 5% of the Light's capacity, now it is possible to reveal much more without fear—with the condition that we restrict accordingly. We are not better than the Israelites who lived 400 years ago. Even when Rav Abraham Azulai revealed that we can study Kabbalah, people didn't suddenly start studying *The Zohar*. But today, in the time of the Messiah, the Light doesn't stop to ask permission; it breaks through and reveals itself. Everywhere the Light hasn't been revealed before, it asserts its intention to be revealed soon. We live in the time of the Messiah, and those who cherish their lives had better prepare for the revelation of Light that is expected to flood the world at any moment. This is the practical meaning of Rav Abraham Azulai's statement regarding the cancellation of the decree. The Light is already here, and it is going to be revealed in a volume, manner, and circumstance that lie beyond our control.

The Ari says that the holiday of *Shavuot* occurs seven weeks after Passover not because that is how it is written in the Torah, but because *Shavuot* is the result of activity occurring in the spiritual world. Nothing in the physical world can be the cause of anything else. The Torah is nothing but a physical tool that contains Light in a coded form. We need the Torah just as we need our physical body—to reveal Light in the material world. During *Shavuot*, the Light is revealed with tremendous force. To prepare for this, it is necessary to count the *Omer*. We count the *Omer* according to all the kabbalistic meditations in order to build a vessel that will enable us to deal successfully with the revelation of *Shavuot*. There is no need for anything else. The Creator wants to bless all of Creation.

Another kabbalistic connection is to make *Kiddush* after the Morning Prayer and to have a dairy meal afterward. This is something that is done only on *Shavuot*, when *Malchut* reaches and touches the *Keter* of *Zeir Anpin*. This is a tremendous jump into the future. By touching the point of origin, we can reach the future and accomplish the removal of death forever. This energy matches the energy of milk, which is connected to the right column: the emanation of

Chesed (mercy), birth, and the life force that erupts and is realized in the world. By eating dairy products, we make a physical action that connects us with the events of *Shavuot* in the upper worlds. Just as flipping the switch turns on the Light in the room, the dairy meal draws the energy of *Shavuot* into our life. It is hard to believe that eating a cheese-filled pastry and drinking chocolate milk can offer us a life portion until the end of the year, but this is the natural law of the universe: Every physical action, even a small one, awakens similar actions in the spiritual world. And these actions, when done with the right timing, can create far-reaching results.

There is a connection between *Shavuot* and *Lag B'Omer*. *Shavuot* and *Lag B'Omer* are dates on which we can receive huge packages of life energy. At *Lag B'Omer*, it is quite simple: Read *The Zohar* as much as possible throughout the night. At *Shavuot* it is also simple, but there are a few more specific instructions. In order to connect to *Keter* of *Zeir Anpin* and to establish the removal of death in our life, we must read a summary of the Torah. We must start from *Beresheet* and read the first three verses and the last three verses in each portion. If the end of a portion is very close to the end of a chapter, we must continue the reading until the end of that chapter. In this manner, we continue throughout the Torah and the Prophets.

There is, however, an exception to this rule. In the portion of *Yitro*, we read, in addition to the first and last three verses, the entire 19th chapter. In *The Book of Exodus*, in the portion of *Mishpatim*, chapter 24, we read from verse 12 to the end of the portion. In *the Book of Leviticus*, in the portion *Va'etchanan*, after the first three verses, we skip to the Ten Utterances and read chapter 5 to the end of the portion. In the portion of *Reeh*, after the first three verses, we skip to chapter 17, verse 9, and from there we read to the end of the portion. In *the Book of Ezekiel*, we read all of chapter 1, and then we skip to the last three verses in the book. If it is all finished before dawn, we open a book of Kabbalah, says The Ari, and complete the night of studying the secrets of the Torah.

Kabbalah is not something new. It is 3,400 years old and was given to us on Mount Sinai. Kabbalah connects us with very old truths; it brings to our consciousness things we already know in our subconscious minds. Only the robotic influences of modern life prevent us from applying these truths with appropriate seriousness in our daily lives. In order to stop being robots, we must fundamentally change and renew our consciousness.

The "acquisition of life insurance" during *Shavuot* is thus accompanied by a decision that we can change the face of the world and ourselves. From now on we will see other human beings as an integral part of ourselves, and we will treat them that way. In our efforts to change and elevate our consciousness, we will move forward until *Rosh Hashanah*, knowing that until then we have been given life without limits. Let us pray that with the revelation of the secret, the Kabbalah, on Mount Sinai, we ourselves can now become the real revelation. We must realize through the power of the revelation that we are one with the Creator. There is no greater truth. At *Shavuot*, we have the opportunity understand it with our minds, connect with it in our hearts, and act on it with every aspect of our being.

Rosh Chodesh Tammuz
(CANCER)

Many people believe that the month of *Tammuz* is first mentioned in the *Book of Ezekiel*, part 8, verse 14—but they are mistaken. In *The Book of Creation*, Abraham the Patriarch discusses at length the month of *Tammuz*, its energy, and its consciousness. The word *Tammuz* is also mentioned in the Torah with regard to the lunar month of that name.

The month of *Tammuz* occurs in midsummer. But its actual time, like that of all the other Lunar months, is bound to the cycle of the moon and the structure of the leap years rather than to the sun cycle. During *Tammuz*, the group of stars indicating the astrological sign of Cancer (the crab) crosses the horizon.

Our ego tries to convince us that we are in total control of our lives, but Kabbalah teaches that we are exposed to external influences from the planets and the astrological signs. This is documented explicitly in *The Zohar* and *The Book of Formation*. Whoever is oblivious to the influence of the planets is literally under their spells and has no more free will than a robot. Fortunately, Abraham the Patriarch has shown us how to control these influences by doing appropriate spiritual work. The information needed to accomplish this is described in *The Book of Formation*. By reading from *The Book of Formation*, we can connect to the source of cosmic energy, and from there we can gain control of the influence of the stars and planets. The month of *Tammuz* is controlled by the energy of the moon, and this energy is channeled to the world in accordance to the consciousness of the astrological sign of Cancer. As Abraham the Patriarch explains, the Aramaic letters created the entire universe. The letter *Tav* ת created the moon, and the letter *Chet* ח created the sign of Cancer. With the use of these two letters, we can therefore control the month of *Tammuz*.

The Zohar, given to Moses on Mount Sinai and studied by Daniel the prophet and Mordechai Ben Yair, also discusses the month of *Tammuz*. In *The Zohar*, in the book *Shmot*, it is written that Yochevet hid Moses for three months when he was a baby. On the surface, this means that Yochevet bore Moses at the sixth month of gestation. The Egyptians knew how to calculate the delivery date of a child, and they even knew the sex of every unborn baby—so they planned to visit Yochevet at the end of the nine months. Since she delivered three months before the expected date, Yochevet hid the baby in a basket without the Egyptians knowing, so that they wouldn't come and kill the baby as had been decreed by Pharaoh.

The Zohar teaches that every story in *The Bible*, including this one, is a code that is designed to show us the secrets of the universe and the concealed laws that govern it. During three months every year—*Tammuz*, *Av*, and *Tevet*—an energy is revealed in the universe that can be harnessed and controlled only through use of very specific tools, without which chaos can easily penetrate the entire world. As disclosed in *The Book of Formation*, *Tammuz* is connected to the astrological sign of Cancer. Surprisingly, this also refers to the disease of the same name. Abraham the Patriarch knew about cancer long before the advent of modern medicine. Abraham also knew in detail the characteristics of the disease and the means by which it could be prevented. A malignant growth spreads without any order, inconsiderate of the environment. This is Satan consciousness, as it appears in the universe during the month of *Tammuz*. Therefore the disease of cancer always starts in the month of *Tammuz*.

No other month of the year is related to this disease. Even the month of *Av*—in which both Holy Temples were destroyed, and during which the holocaust of the Spanish Jews in the hands of the inquisition began—is not called the month of the disasters or the month of the diseases. Only *Tammuz* is related to the most threatening and frightening one of all. Anyone stricken by cancer feels as if an enemy has invaded and feels that there is no power to stop it. And what about all the people born in this month? They are connected to the sign of cancer in their *Keter* emanation. Are they more vulnerable to the disease because of it? As we know, Aramaic names and words contain their energetic essence and therefore are self-explanatory. So let's consider the word *cancer* in order to better understand the essence of the disease and the month with which it is connected.

The word cancer in Aramaic is *Sartan*, which is a combination of two other words, *Sar* and *Tan*. *Sar* means to remove, eliminate, and clean. *Tan* is an Aramaic word that deals with different aspects of chaos; the word *Tina* (hatred), which is one of its derivatives, connects physical chaos and destruction with negative feelings such as sorrow, anger, and frustration. Rav Shimon and The Ari explain that these feelings separate us from the Light and happiness, dropping us like a ripe fruit directly into the arms of the Angel of Death. Therefore the name of the month, *Sartan*, actually refers to "removing sorrow."

The name the Creator gave the sign controlling the month of *Tammuz* includes a clear instruction on how to deal with the excess Light revealed in this month, how to prevent the sickness connected to *Tammuz*, and how to prevent any appearance of chaos in the world—including events on the scale of a Temple destruction, the holocaust of the European community, and a world war.

Why did the Creator initiate a reality in which both good and evil act simultaneously? There is a simple answer: A world in which good and evil coexist is essential to the removal of Bread of Shame and the presence of free choice. When the first man bit into the forbidden fruit, he lowered himself—and the entire world—from the consciousness of the Tree of Life, and in its place he manifested the Tree of Knowledge of Good and Evil. The Creator is responsible for everything good that happens to us. We humans are responsible for all the rest—for everything negative that takes place anywhere in the universe. But we can and should look at this situation from an optimistic point of view: We live in a world that is not entirely bad, but also good. The Creator guides us to remove the bad so that we can enjoy the good.

Why is the universe flooded with so much energy during the month of *Tammuz*? The answer lies in the stars. As we know, every month in the year is governed by a planet and a sign. The energy of the month emanates from the planet and is passed to us through a filter, the sign. Ten months of the year are governed by five planets, and each one of these planets—Saturn, Jupiter, Mars, Venus, and Mercury—divides its energy between two signs. During two months of the year, however, this is not the case: Only the sun controls the month of *Av*, and only the moon controls the month of *Tammuz*. This is the reason for the strong energy of judgment in the world during the months of *Av* and *Tammuz*. But the abundance of Light and the level of judgment don't necessarily mean damage, pain, or suffering for us. It all depends on the level of affinity between the Light and the vessel—an affinity that we ourselves can control.

The most problematic period starts on the 17th of *Tammuz* and ends on the ninth of *Av*. This period is the most dangerous with respect to accidents or diseases like cancer. How do we know this? It is because the month of *Tammuz* is governed by the sign of Cancer, the energy of Tan—sorrow, darkness, and chaos. As King David said, "The skies tell of his honor." The skies tell us what the Creator does.

But perhaps we might ask, Why did the Creator concentrate so much energy into these two months of *Tammuz* and *Av*? The answer is simple: Because this is exactly what we need. Whoever connects to the Light in the right way, thereby expanding his spiritual vessel, receives in these months an additional life force that gives him a better chance to deal with the rest of the year. We learn this from the 17th day of the month of *Tammuz*. It was on this day that Moses brought the two tablets, after the Torah was given on Mount Sinai. Moses came down the mountain with an instrument that could manifest the end of death in this world. This is the instrument that was later placed in the tabernacle, and it was one that was meant for the benefit of all the people of the world. On the 17th of *Tammuz*, when Moses descended the mountain and saw the Golden Calf that the Israelites had built, the tablets broke. On that day, Moses brought to the world immortality and complete freedom from chaos. He established a pure connection to the energy of the Tree of Life. As we know, in order to reveal life in this world, there must be a connection between body and soul. When a person dies, his soul lifts up and leaves his body. On the 17th of *Tammuz*, Moses brought the means by which the physical body could be injected with the quantity and quality of Light that brings the body a total connection with the soul consciousness— a connection that is eternal, and one that cannot be severed. In this way, death is eradicated forever. This is the true essence of the 17th of *Tammuz*.

But the question remains, Why was the 17th of *Tammuz* chosen as the day for the injection of life force into the physical world? What is special about this day? Again, in the lunar date—as in the name and as in every word of the Torah—there is a hidden code. This day was chosen because since the time of Creation, it has contained a unique intelligent energy force that is precisely suited to this mission. *Tov* טוֹב (good) has the numerical value of 17. It is the best day for revealing the best energy. And since nothing disappears in the spiritual realm, this good energy of permanent connection to the Tree of Life returns to be revealed each year.

Moses connected to this energy and actually attained eternal life. That is why it is written in *The Zohar* that "Moses didn't die." Now it is up to us to complete his mission and connect ourselves to that energy. This is a day of energetic short circuits, troubles, and disasters—but only to those who don't deserve to receive the Light. Whoever chooses to build himself a Golden Calf rather than connecting with certainty, awe, and love to the Torah—whoever chooses to see the different and the fragments instead of the unity, whoever doesn't bother to practice loving thy neighbor as thyself—invites on this day the breaking of the walls and the beginning of the destruction. But we must always remember that the good came first; this is the choice of the cosmic failure. Only if the vessel is not appropriate for the Light will the world be damaged. It is true that we don't know for sure when the vessel is ready and worthy, but we certainly know that in the month of *Tammuz* we have a cosmic opportunity to remove *Tan* from our midst; to be cleansed of any negativity and any type of imbalance; to be immunized against any type of cancer, be it physical or spiritual; and to gain a tremendous injection of Light and energy that will bring us closer to the Tree of Life.

The animal called *sartan* (crab) and is associated with the sign of Cancer. It always walks sideways, never forward or back. But what is the significance of this? If we analyze this kind of movement, we will realize that unlike forward or backward movement, it is not continuous. If we try to walk like the crab, we bring the right leg to the left leg. We will stand, and only then will we move the left leg to the left. The message embodied in the crab is therefore one of discontinuity. As long as we prevent the continuous flow of Light through us, we will expose ourselves to the danger of sickness and disasters. But if we strive to flow with the Light, we will enable happiness, completion, and freedom to manifest in our lives. Continuity means endless, immortality, a total connection with the Tree of Life. Stopping creates space. Whoever dwells in sadness in the month of *Tammuz* puts his soul in danger and risks exposure to the disease of cancer.

What is the meaning of the name *Tammuz*? Why was the moon chosen to influence its spiritual Light in this month? In *the Book of Yecheskel* it is written, "And he brought me to the gates of the house of God, which is to the North, and there the women are sitting, crying for *Tammuz*."

The commentators relate this passage to idol worshipping, meaning that *Tammuz* is a Babylonian god, and it was customary to cry for its death during the month of *Tammuz*. But what is the meaning of the location and the women? The commentators have no answer to that. *Tammuz* תמוז is composed of the two words: *Tam* תם and *Uz* וז (*Uz* in Aramaic is written with the letters *Vav* ו and *Zain* ז). The sign of Taurus was created by the letter *Vav*. The sign of Gemini was created by the letter *Zain*. *Tammuz* comes after these two months have ended, and with it ends their spiritual influence.

The sign of Taurus occurs on the month of *Iyar*, the month of healing. A tremendous Light, raw and unrestrained, descends on the world during this month in order to help us remove chaos from our lives. If there is no fit vessel to receive the Light, catastrophes can occur, such as the plague that killed 24,000 of Rav Akiva's students. Unlike the month of *Tammuz*, in *Iyar* there is no protective device. Therefore we never start a new business, we don't marry, and we don't purchase new things in *Iyar*.

The sign of Gemini is the month of *Sivan*, an air sign. Air represents consciousness of central column and restriction, balance, and harmony. Among the three air signs, Libra represents the right column of the center column; Aquarius represents the left column of the central column; and

Gemini represents the central column of the central column. This is one of the reasons Gemini was chosen for the "giving" of the Torah. When the revelation on Mount Sinai occurred, all the universe was in balance. That is why the Israelites were able to survive the event and the world was not destroyed despite the tremendous Light that was revealed—a Light that was meant to balance the negativity of the world and bring forth a state of death to death.

Every month contains the seed of the month that precedes it. If we create in *Sivan* "the death of death, forever," then we can execute it during *Tammuz*. The aspect of Gemini creates a sort of spiritual ozone layer and thus helps balance the unrestrained Light that descends on the world on *Iyar*, at the same time preparing the world for salvation. Moses came down from Mount Sinai on the 17th of *Tammuz* holding the Torah—the complete expression of raw energy and its balancing factor, the energy and consciousness of restriction. *Tammuz* means that the time has come for the complete revelation of the force in the letters *Vav* and *Zain*. This is the meaning of the month of *Tammuz*, and that is why it occurs after the months of *Iyar* and *Sivan*.

The third month of concealment is *Tevet*, the sign of Capricorn. Seemingly, there is no justification here for a dangerous excess of energy. But even so, there is clear proof that there is tremendous energy on this month: On the 10th of *Tevet*, the siege on Jerusalem started. Saturn is a massive star, and it expresses its capability to project powerful spiritual energy. If we list the three months by the strength of their radiation, then *Tevet*, which is fed by Saturn, is the weakest of the three. *Av*, which is fed by the sun, is the strongest one, and on it both Holy Temples were destroyed. The Temple is surrounded by defensive walls, just like an onion; as we move away from the center, the walls become weaker. When the universe contains energy equal to the strength of the walls, and when people cause that energy to manifest in a negative way, that energy can break the wall. As the energy revealed increases, it becomes possible to break stronger walls and come closer to the heart of the atomic reactor that feeds the world. We thus have an opportunity during these three months to break through the *klipot* (barriers) that surround our inner Light, the soul, and allow this potential Light to manifest in our lives. We become our life and not have our life rule us. This is the secret of these three months, during which Yochevet hid Moses in the basket.

The Zohar teaches us that a person is a microcosm that reflects the entire universe. Like everything else in the universe, man is built from two main components: the body consciousness and the soul consciousness. The body consciousness—the desire to receive for the self alone—instills in us the illusion of limitations. The soul consciousness, a Godlike part, is free and unlimited.

How much can we strengthen the soul consciousness and empower it over the body consciousness? Therein lies the entire secret. Any problem or hardship we experience is connected to the short circuits we created in past lives. Any difficult event is an opportunity to clean negative energy we collected in the past and to correct the defects. Whoever falls prey to depression because of hardships ensures only that when he returns in the next life, he will have to endure the same problems again and again.

Depression is connected to the desire to receive for the self alone, and therefore it alienates a person from the Light. This disconnection from the Light prevents the person from understanding and analyzing his situation in the right way, hindering him from finding solutions to his problems. By contrast, a person who is connected to the positive consciousness sees hardship as an opportunity to reveal Light and therefore is not afraid of picking the glove. Such a person will always tell the Light, even in the hard times, Thank you, there must be a good reason; please give me more, even if it hurts right now. The body wants to receive: food, drink, rest, and much more. The soul doesn't need any of these.

The Ari, Rav Shimon, and Abraham the Patriarch teach us techniques with which to control our destiny. In the course of our lives, we will always face challenges and will be tested. We will be exposed to situations in which the illusion of loss of control will grow stronger. It is important to remember, however, that this is only an illusion. Cancer is not a matter of luck. With the Light, we can remove any drop or seed of cancer, anger, and chaos from ourselves, and merit the balanced connection to the Tree of Life.

Rosh Chodesh Av
(LEO)

The month of *Av* is a special time. During this month, we are privy to the means and ways in which to control our destiny and remove chaos from the world through an especially strong connection to the Light of the Creator. On *Rosh Chodesh*, we are able to connect to all the potential and positive energy intelligence connected to the month. In order to do this, we learn about the month, as we remember *The Zohar*'s lesson from *Beresheet*: knowledge is the connection.

Av draws on the spiritual Light generated by the sun. After passing through the filter known as the sign of Leo, this Light affects all the events that transpire during the month. We draw this wisdom from *The Book of Formation*, the most ancient source of astrological and kabbalistic wisdom.

There we read:

> He appointed the letter *Chaf* כ and bestowed it with a crown and to it assigned the Sun, Wednesday, and the left ear.... He appointed the letter *Tet* ט and bestowed it with a crown and assigned to it the constellation of Leo, the month of *Av*, and the vertebrae.

The sun—the center of the solar system—was created by the energy encapsulated in the letter *Chaf* כ, and the group of stars in the constellation of Leo was created by the energy encapsulated in the letter *Tet* ט. In the same way that our body was created on the basis of formation of molecular DNA, the sun, the sign of Leo, and the month of *Av* were created from the DNA made up of the letters of the month: *Chaf* and *Tet*. Abraham the Patriarch reveals to us that only through the essence of the letters of the month can we control our destiny—a merit that we received on the day we were born.

The signature qualities of the sign of Leo are leadership, initiative, and control. These qualities shine on all of us during the month of *Av* and aid us in achieving control in our daily lives. Only by manifesting these qualities and controlling our lives is it possible for us to begin to understand the surroundings in which we live. Our situation can be likened to a businessman who must survey the market and learn not only who his competitors are, but what powers and trends affect the market—after which he storms the market, trying to conquer and control one sector or another. Our ego plants within us the illusion that we control our lives, but in order to control death, business, and health, we must first become acquainted with the facts of life, learn the rules of the game, and understand our environment at its foundation.

With the onset of the 21st century, we expect to see a great change in the lives of all people. This change comes from our entrance into the age of Kabbalah. Just as people disregarded the Internet and did not anticipate its prosperity, those who disregard Kabbalah and the essence of the Torah can expect a similar surprise. The Internet is the *Sfirah* of *Malchut* of the Information Age, and the exposure of the wisdom of Kabbalah is *Keter* of the Consciousness Age—an age in which we will achieve better lives, free of negativity.

According to conventional religion, the Creator is responsible for producing miracles in the world, while we are completely passive. According to Kabbalah, the responsibility to produce miracles rests on our shoulders. The Creator provides us with the power and the tools, but the decision to cause a miracle to occur lies in our hands. One of these tools is the planet Jupiter, whose nature produced the miracles of *Chanukah* and *Purim* for our forefathers. By connecting to Jupiter's internal energy, the ability to create miracles exists even today. Rav Shimon Bar Yochai wrote in *The Zohar* that only after 2,000 years—meaning in our time—will the true significance of the Revelation on Mount Sinai emerge. And the truth began to emerge nearly 80 years ago, when Rav Ashlag began his life's work: writing his "Ladder" commentary and translation of *The Zohar* and founding The Kabbalah Centre. It is natural that any effort to change a 3,400-year-old tradition will meet with opposition. Despite this opposition, however, we find ourselves at the end of an era in which people allowed their destinies to be determined by others. We will no longer place our lives in the hands of surgeons or our businesses in the hands of lawyers and bankers. In the Age of Aquarius, the 21st century, every one of us will take responsibility and manage our own lives—for that is the only way to transform a history that has been paved with chaos into one of prosperity and harmony.

Traditionally, *Av* is considered a negative month. Throughout this month in history, both Holy Temples were destroyed; in 1492, the document was signed to officially expel the Spanish Jews during the Inquisition; and in 1942 the Final Solution was implemented by Nazi Germany. God seems especially angry during *Av*. Therefore, we are told not to begin anything important in this month: no marriages, no opening of businesses, and no acquisition of property. We are also told to refrain from celebration and holidays out of respect for the Destruction. Yet if *Av* is so negative, why did the Talmudic sages appoint *Tisha B'Av* (the ninth day of *Av*) as a holiday? It seems illogical. But the wisdom of Kabbalah reveals to us that on *Tisha B'Av*, the consciousness of Messiah comes to the world because the ninth day is connected to the *Sfirah* of *Yesod* and the reproductive organs. And what is born on this day? The internal consciousness of Leo, also expressed in the numerology of the constellation's name: *Aryeh* אריה (lion) is numerically equal to 216, the number of letters in the 72 Names of God! Messiah consciousness is therefore an expression of the thought consciousness concealed in the 72 Names of God that were used to split the Red Sea and achieve mind over matter.

Kabbalah teaches that the Creator is only and purely the benefactor of His creations. Damage comes to the world because of a vessel's incapacity to contain and conduct the Light. If a person puts his finger into an electrical socket, he does not blame the Creator of the universe. In order to remove the veil that stands in the way of our karmic process, we must have a consciousness of true concern for others. A few of the world's wealthiest people have expressed this sentiment, indicating that humanity's consciousness is developing in the right direction. Still, it is heartening to see many engaging in *Tikkun Hanefesh* (correction of the soul) during *Ana Bekoach*. Nevertheless, Rav Ashlag emphasizes that it is especially important to meditate on others during this prayer in the broadest possible sense, and not only for ourselves, our family, and our friends. The Light of the Creator—a spark, a part of God above—can be found in all of us. Therefore, in order to love ourselves, we must love all of mankind.

On the 15th of the month, we come to the peak of opportunity to connect in a balanced way to the totality of the Light of the Creator that is prepared for us by *Zeir Anpin*. On *Tu B'Av* (the 15th day of *Av*), harmony reigns throughout the universe between every vessel and the Light. That is why it is a happy day, and one that is perfect for discovering soul mates, finding business partners, signing contracts, and making new beginnings (see the chapter on *Tu B'Av* page 255).

The month of *Av* is therefore the greatest opportunity of the year to draw the Light of the Creator and, in so doing, to remove chaos from the world. Darkness is removed by Light, not by gunfire. The quantum effect—the law of spiritual unity among all creations—promises that the more people learn Kabbalah and reveal Light in the world, the better all of our lives will be. This law reveals to us the tremendous responsibility weighing on our shoulders: The destiny of all mankind and the entire universe rests in the hands of each and every one of us.

The Fifth of Av — THE DEATH ANNIVERSARY OF RAV ISAAC LURIA (THE ARI)

Rav Isaac Luria, The *Ari Hakadosh*, died on *Hei B'Av* (the fifth day of *Av*) in 1574. We are accustomed to associating death with sadness and mourning, but the *hilulah* (death anniversary) of a *tzadik* (righteous person) is a paradox. On the one hand, the day a righteous person dies is considered a happy one for reasons we shall explain. On the other hand, there is no doubt that we would be happy to have The Ari physically here with us today. We would then be able, for example, to ask him questions about the future, for he was able to see and know all after he had learned the tremendous depth and scope of Kabbalah.

The Ari was born in Jerusalem and as a child moved with his mother to Egypt to live with his uncle. He lived in Egypt for 13 years, spending most of his time alone along the shores of the Nile. During this time, he attained levels of spiritual enlightenment and understanding that led him to Tsefat to teach Rav Chaim Vital the secrets of Kabbalah and, by doing so, passing this wisdom on to future generations.

In the *Kitvei H'Ari* (The Ari's Writings), Rav Chaim Vital writes:

> These are the things that my teacher said regarding the root of my soul. On *Rosh Chodesh Adar* 1571, he told me that while he was in Egypt, he began to understand his own destiny, and to understand the upper worlds and true reality. There it was said to him that he would come to the city of Tsefat where I live in order to teach me the wisdom of Kabbalah. And he told me that he did not come to live in Tsefat for any other purpose, and not only that, but the entire reason for this incarnation was to teach me, to complete me and not for his own needs, because he did not need to come. He also told me that he is not charged with teaching anyone other than myself. And when I complete the study for which he came to this world, he will no longer need to exist in this world.

This passage reveals that at the moment Rav Chaim Vital finished his studies with The Ari, The Ari's job in this world would be complete, and he would immediately return to the World of Truth. Therefore The Ari did not die, but simply left our physical world. We are unable to see him at present, but as Rav Abraham Azulai explained, this will change beginning in the year 5760/2000. Rav Chaim Vital's study included the wisdom necessary for us today in order to bring the collective consciousness to the level of Messiah. This means that the wealth of knowledge revealed by the *Kitvei Ha'Ari* enable the masses to understand their destinies. At the moment The Ari finished passing this wisdom on to Rav Chaim Vital, there was no purpose to his continued existence in the physical world.

Rav Chaim Vital merited some 200 possessions of other souls in his lifetime, but he was not permitted to complete his tikun with The Ari in this way. That is why The Ari took on human form but did not actually need to come into the world for his own sake. Consequently, The Ari died at age 38. It is quite clear from this story that The Ari did not die of an illness that plagued Tsefat. The Ari came to this world only to teach us the secrets of Kabbalah by means of Rav Chaim Vital, and the moment he completed this task, he no longer had a reason to remain in this world.

We know that The Ari's message was especially intended for our time. It was approximately 80 years ago, when Rav Ashlag established The Kabbalah Centre in 1922 and began to promulgate *The Zohar* and The Ari, that the layperson finally had the opportunity to understand The Ari. This wisdom had remained concealed for over 400 years, and even the wisest of sages found The Ari's writings difficult to decipher. Today, thanks to Rav Ashlag, anyone can learn and understand Kabbalah the way it was taught during the times of Rav Shimon and The Ari.

Rav Chaim Vital continues:

> He (The Ari) also told me that my soul was above with a few supernal angels, great in supernal purpose and the only way I could go any further would be through my actions.

Here The Ari reveals that in order to connect with the seed of our souls, we must perform spiritual work. It all depends on our actions. The Ari himself lived like a pauper in a meager hut along the Nile until he merited his enlightenment, regardless of the fact that he had been raised in a wealthy home. His behavior did not reflect his wealth, nor did he act better than those of lesser stature. He had actually exhausted his spiritual work until he finally merited the completion of his life's purpose. The Ari understood that money is just an expression of the Light of the Creator and was not designed to increase the ego that traps all of us. The Ari elevated beyond body consciousness, which is the consciousness of the desire to receive for the self alone. We learn in *Parashat Noach*, "Man's inclination is evil from his youth." The moment our souls incarnate into physical bodies, they connect with the consciousness of the desire to receive for the self alone, with evil. The body is inherently evil.

A truly good person differs from a seemingly good person when he is faced with choosing between his own personal benefit and that of others. If a person is willing to sacrifice himself and give his life for someone else, he rises above the limitation of individuality and overcomes his body consciousness. This kind of action expresses not only the consciousness of sharing, but also the truths of giving up physical gratification. There are people who are naturally inclined to share, and there are also those whose sole purpose in life is to receive for themselves alone. The years that The Ari spent in Egypt were dedicated to the process of purifying his consciousness, overcoming the aspect of physicality in his life, converting his desire to receive, and completing his life process, which was the sharing of the secrets of Kabbalah. This was the condition for teaching Kabbalah without which The Ari could not have taught Rav Chaim Vital. The Ari revealed to Rav Chaim Vital that his soul had reached the highest possible place—even higher than that of some angels. Because The Ari was Rav Chaim Vital's teacher, we can see that The Ari's soul was even higher than that, and his soul was rooted in a higher place than we can possibly imagine.

Accordingly, The Ari had no difficulty in seeing Rav Chaim Vital's previous incarnations or the process that he had to go through:

> He showed me that which I have to correct now in this incarnation: I must disclose the wisdom of *The Zohar*. And he told me that my being an incarnation of the Magid Mishneh, I was a great fountain of wisdom, and very wise.

That is why I am not heavily in pursuit of personal wisdom, because my aforementioned incarnations are only concerned with my own soul.

In other words, The Ari reveals that in all of Rav Chaim Vital's previous incarnations, he was an intellectual only for the sake of his soul. "From the point of view of *Ruach* and *Neshama*, there are other things incarnating!" Here The Ari explains that a spiritual person is someone who has come in his *tikkun* process to the level of *Ruach*, and has completely disconnected from the level of *Nefesh* and the desire to receive for the self alone. This level is more specific and strict, whereas anyone can call himself or herself a "spiritual person." It does not matter how many years a person learns Kabbalah or any other spiritual philosophy. As long as we do not transform our desire to receive for the self alone into a desire to share, we are not worthy of calling ourselves spiritual people.

The Ari continues and reveals that when Rav Chaim Vital was 13 years old, the soul of Rav Elazar Ben Arach, a student of Rav Yochanan Ben Zakkai, came to rest upon him. Incidentally, the two of them are buried side by side in Tiberias. The number 13 is no coincidence either. This is the age at which a person is first given the opportunity to rise above being a child, whose consciousness is only the desire to receive for the self alone. It is a key level in developing the ability to share and care for others, on the way to the level of Ruach. It is difficult to conceive the level of Rav Chaim

Vital's soul, if at the age of only 13 he merited receiving the soul of Rav Elazar Ben Arach, Rav Yochanan Ben Zakkai's student.

The Ari teaches us that it is impossible to realize our potential without practical spiritual work, as Rav Chaim Vital continues to explain how The Ari told him of his many incarnations:

> And he told me that I had to incarnate into this current body because I did not previously believe fully in the wisdom of *The Zohar*. And from his words I understood that I was the *Magid Mishneh* but he did not want to reveal this.

The Ari was not limited by time or space or incarnation. Therefore he could see how damage in one incarnation affected the soul in another incarnation. We are trying to emulate The Ari and achieve a similar level—one beyond time, space, and motion.

It is important to remember that The Kabbalah Centre *Siddur* (Prayer Book) is the means by which we can connect to The Ari and bring him close to us. As we have learned from *The Zohar* and the *Talmud*, when we learn from a particular teacher's lessons, that study alone connects us with the teacher who led us to it. The more we implement the teacher's lessons in our lives, the more we connect to that teacher. In the *Siddur*, The Ari has given us a meditation that especially helps us connect to The Ari's ability to rise above the limitations of time: *Hashem melech, Hashem malach, Hashem yimloch le'olam va'ed*. Traditionally, this verse describes the everlasting nature of the Creator; He ruled, He rules, and He will rule forever. The Ari reveals the connection between these words and the five final Aramiac letters מ ן ץ ף ך to the secret of rising above the frame of time that is expected during the days of Messiah. The Ari explains to us that during the days of Messiah, we will not be limited by an intellectual knowledge and understanding of the past, present, and future. We will actually be able to see them all before our very eyes.

On the first of the intermediary (*Chol Hamo'ed*) days of *Pesach* of the same year, The Ari and Rav Chaim Vital went to a town called Achbara while touring the gravesites of the righteous in the area, whereupon The Ari united the souls of Rav Chaim Vital and Rav Yanai, a *tzadik* (righteous person) who had passed away 1,500 years earlier. While The Ari was talking to Rav Chaim Vital, they suddenly heard Rav Yanai's voice saying, "I am buried in this grave!" The Ari confirmed this and said to Rav Chaim Vital, "You should know that the dead speak the truth, and this is where he is buried. I brought you here to introduce you to one another, and from now on Rav Yanai's soul will be with you wherever you go." Rav Yanai spoke again to The Ari: "This is what the blessed Creator has said. Go and tell this man, Chaim Vital, who is with you, that he has within him an aspect of slander, and his soul is hindered because of it." Rav Yanai told The Ari that Rav Chaim Vital had to correct his character in the area of evil speech and to increase his degree of humility. "And I will be with him everywhere he goes," continued Rav Yanai. "That day, my teacher also told me that my soul belonged and cleaved to the soul of Moses." The Ari was an incarnation of Rav Shimon Bar Yochai, who was an incarnation of Moses. Accordingly, The Ari described the nature of the connection between himself and Rav Chaim Vital, whose souls shared the same root of Moses: "For all souls were included in his soul, especially the souls of the righteous."

Here The Ari teaches us that all souls were included in Moses' soul. As it is known, the soul does not have physical size, and therefore it has no trouble including all existing souls in the soul of a single body. On the other hand, only people like Rav Shimon Bar Yochai, The Ari, and Rav Chaim Vital were able to understand Moses and connect to his mighty soul, and that is why they merited having him incarnate within them for the sole purpose of spreading of Kabbalah and leading future generations in doing so. Not all of us can understand the wide breadth of meaning of Kabbalah, and that is why none of us can single-handedly be responsible for the promulgation of Kabbalah. Rav Shimon and The Ari could speak to people who lived 1,000 years earlier in the same way they would speak to those who will live in the year 2300. The Ari dictated his wisdom to Rav Chaim Vital alone, because only he was able to go to the depths of his mind and pass on things exactly as he heard them. But at that time, The Ari had not yet discussed the ideas of *Ruach* and *Neshama*.

We read in *Sha'ar HaGilgulim (The Gate of Reincarnation)*:

> I also traveled once with my teacher to the place where Rabbi Shimon and his companions gathered, where they did the "*Idra Rabba.*" And there, east of the road (in the cave) there is a solitary rock within which there are two large gaps. The gap on the north side is where Rabbi Shimon sat in the *Idra*.

The Ari was able to identify the energetic imprint that Rav Shimon left 1,500 years before he left the physical place where he sat in the cave. In *Sha'ar HaGilgulim*, it continues:

> And in the gap on the south side, that is where Rabbi Abba (who wrote *The Zohar* from Rabbi Shimon's words) sat. And by the tree opposite the two gaps in the west, that is where Rabbi Elazar sat.

From this description, it is clear that The Ari actually saw what took place at the *Idra Rabba* without the limitations that time imposes on us. The Ari could connect with the members of the *Idra Rabba* as though they had never died—as though they had only left the physical realm. All the *tzadikim* are happy to respond to our invitation, to join us and support us in every aspect of our spiritual work—in our personal and global *tikkun* process toward the World of Truth to which we are headed.

This is the description in *Sha'ar HaGilgulim*:

> He alluded as to why The Ari was chosen as the channel for the knowledge that decodes the secrets of *The Zohar* for the people, after 1,500 years of concealment. The Ari was an incarnation of Rav Shimon Bar Yochai's soul, and that is why he continued doing Rav Shimon's work.

Rav Moshe Cordovero, who lived at the same time in Tsefat, also wrote his own interpretation of *The Zohar*, called *Or Yakar*—Precious Light. The Ari certified that the ideas in his book are correct and true, but The Ari told Rav Chaim Vital that in the Age of Aquarius, 400 years later, the *Kitvei Ha'Ari* and not *Or Yakar* would be used as the basis for *The Zohar*'s consumption by the masses, for the spiritual awakening and spread of Messiah consciousness across the globe—first on an individual level and, ultimately, on a global level. That is why Rav Ashlag, the founder of The Kabbalah Centre, based his writings, called *Hasulam*, or The Ladder, and the *Ten Luminous Emanations* on The Ari's writings rather than on *Or Yakar*. The Ari illustrated his ability to rise above the confines of time, not only for past events but also for future ones. "And I, Chaim Vital, sat in the southern gap, and who sat there before me I did not know." This description reveals a kabbalistic secret to reaching higher levels of consciousness.

In order to reach a higher level of consciousness, we must go through this paradox: To reach certainty, we must first be convinced that nothing is certain. In order to know, we must first be totally convinced that we know nothing. Only when we fulfill this difficult condition do we find ourselves on the path to certainty. The physical aspect of our existence bars us from the possibility of actualizing our total consciousness, including the full intensity of our true reality. The limitations of the five senses and the mind compel us toward nothing but uncertainty. Nevertheless, when we are enlightened by this fact and approach it with certainty, the Light enters our lives. Without Light we have no existence, and our knowledge then bears no significance.

Rav Chaim Vital is grateful for not knowing why he chose to sit in that spot, whereupon The Ari reveals to him that it was Rav Abba's seat. This incident shows us not only that Rav Chaim Vital related to The Ari in the same way that Rav Abba related to Rav Shimon, but that Rav Chaim Vital's soul is connected to that of Rav Abba. Because Rav Chaim Vital's purpose was not intellectual, he had to rely on the Light, and it had to come from his energetic quality. After this event, Rav Chaim Vital would bring his son, Rav Shmuel Vital, to the world, and he would commit The Ari's words to writing just as Rav Abba had done with Rav Shimon's writings in his time. Why did Rav Chaim Vital feel the need to sit precisely on that southern rock? The answer is written as follows: "One of the members of the *Idra Rabba* is from the root of my soul, and it is Rabbi Abba." Rav Chaim Vital reveals that he did not choose to be the scribe for The Ari's writings, that he did not do it for the historical honor he would receive, but only because it was his life's purpose. He had no choice, because his soul's root was connected to Rav Abba's soul. Just as Rav Abba brought *The Zohar* to fruition, Rav Chaim Vital brought to Light its sequel compilation: the explanation of *The Zohar*, also known as the *Kitvei Ha'Ari*.

Spiritual consciousness does not translate into mental power except when we let the Light guide us. Does this mean that the spiritual path is simply observing *Shabbat* and waiting for the Light to enter and lay us upon the path we long for—to our *tikkun*? Absolutely not. The Ari could have revealed Rav Chaim Vital's destiny to him in Tsefat. Instead, however, he chose to walk with him for two hours to the Idra Rabba—to an experience that would lend understanding of his own life's purpose. If this is the case, what do we need to do to have these sorts of experiences? We must remain active and not spare ourselves any effort. Rav Chaim Vital had the merit to be The Ari's student, but in *The Zohar* it is written that in the time of Messiah there will no longer be the need for teachers, because all of us will be connected to the Light, young and old alike. How is this possible? Today, many students of Kabbalah don't even know how to read Aramaic, so how can they understand the secrets of Kabbalah? The answer to this question is found in Rav Chaim Vital's words: "Without even knowing it." The connection to the Light and to all the secrets of Kabbalah do not come from intellect and cannot be learned in universities, but can be found only by connecting to the source of spiritual energy: the Light of the Creator and the souls of the righteous that have brought the wisdom of Kabbalah to the world.

The tool for a successful connection lies in the soul pulsing through our bodies. All of our souls were present at the Revelation on Mount Sinai, and therefore all know the secrets of Kabbalah. All we need are whatever physical actions that connect us with our soul's source and raise our consciousness to another level. The energetic imprint left by Rav Abba was enough to awaken Rav Chaim Vital to the consciousness that was inherent in his soul. *The Zohar* tells us that Aramaic was the only language spoken in the world before the Tower of Babel incident. Have we forgotten this information? Obviously not, because the soul does not "forget." How can we connect to the information concealed in the depths of our soul? By reading *The Zohar*. This action connects us to the wisdom found in our soul in the same way that surfing the "Net" connects us with information found in sites around the world. We do not know ahead of time what is going to happen when we get to those sites; we only know how to get to them. It is much the same with our work.

We know how to establish the spiritual connection and how to awaken the soul within us. With tools such as *The Zohar* and the *Kitvei H'Ari*, spiritual trips to gravesites of *tzadikim* on their death anniversaries, and participation in the cosmic programs of *Shabbat* and the holidays, we can succeed in connecting with our souls and revealing and knowing our personal mission. This connection also provides us access to information that has existed in the depths of our vast souls for hundreds and thousands of years. Knowledge of Hebrew or Aramaic is unnecessary. The soul already knows everything. In these connections we are not using our minds, but rather bridging the gap between the material world and the world of truth. Tools like the *Brich Shmae*, which we recite on *Shabbat*, connect us to the 99% consciousness—the consciousness of the mind and the senses—with the perfect truth that is found beyond the confines of their performance. We are converting the 1% consciousness so that it can unite with its true essence.

Every time we cite a *tzadik*, we merit that his soul attaches to ours. By means of reading his writings, we all connect with The Ari and merit his help and guidance.

Anyone starting to learn Kabbalah is actually beginning a path toward the revelation of powerful knowledge that is capable of removing chaos from our lives, despite the fact that few students are actually aware of or comprehend this. We are accustomed to doubting all the answers to our problems with the claim of "it's too good to be true." This is the trademark of the last 3,400 years. Since we have yet to see our lives free of chaos, it is difficult to imagine such a situation. And through Kabbalah, chaos belongs only to the world of illusion, while order and harmony belong to the world of truth.

Just when The Ari was about to pass on, Rav Chaim Vital left the room, and Rav Isaac HaCohen entered. The Ari asked, "Where did Chaim go? Why did he leave me now of all times?" And Rav Yitzchak was sorry that Rav Chaim Vital had left, for he then understood that The Ari wanted to relate concealed wisdom to his beloved student. So Rav Yitzchak said, "What are we to do from now on?" To which The Ari responded, "Tell all of my students that from today onward, they shall not connect with the wisdom I have taught them, for they did not understand it properly. Only Rav Chaim Vital will connect with it, as long as it is in secret." The Ari added, "And if you are worthy, I will come and teach you." And his soul left with a kiss.

Tisha B'Av
(9TH OF LEO)

According to conventional religious thinking, *Tisha B'Av* is a meaningful only because it is the day on which the Temples were destroyed. But a physical event cannot be a cause because the physical world itself is purely an effect. The cause of anything in the material universe can only exist on the spiritual level. On *Tisha B'Av*, negativity has total dominion; chaos reigns over all creation. This is the day on which the Holy Temple was destroyed. Yet because Light and darkness cannot exist in the same place, the only day on which chaos can be removed from the world or the Holy Temple can be destroyed is on *Tisha B'Av*. This is the great paradox of the holiday, and also its great importance. At times, chaos has ruled on *Tisha B'Av*, but great Light can also be revealed on that day—a Light that can enable the birth of Messiah. We gather on *Tisha B'Av* to reveal this great Light in the world and to drive out all aspects of chaos from the entire universe. It is therefore unfortunate that *Tisha B'Av* is ignored by so many people.

One of Rav Brandwein's greatest lessons is: Pay attention to things that seem to lack importance, and take notice of the moments during the prayer service when people choose to take a break or chat with their neighbor. Those seemingly meaningless things and times reveal the greatest Light of all. One such time is *Tisha B'Av*.

Kabbalah teaches that the Creator's intention on *Tisha B'Av* is exactly the opposite of what we think. Here we have a chance to destroy the source and seed of all chaos by our own means. This special opportunity comes only once a year, because on this day alone there is total presence of all aspects of negative consciousness. The enemy is concentrated into one place, so we may completely destroy the enemy in one fell swoop. The month of *Av* is the month of absolute Light or absolute darkness. The ninth day of the month expresses the foundation of this totality. The collection of all these things together creates a brighter picture of what can take place this day on the spiritual plane.

Let us now address the significance of the letter *Tet*'s control over the month of *Av*, especially on *Tisha B'Av*. *Tet* represents the dwelling place, the ingathering of all those who were, are, and who will never be. When we speak about *Tisha B'Av* and the Light of Messiah, we are talking about the final and complete effect of all those souls. At the point in which Messiah will be revealed, all Light must also be revealed in the world. This will be the completion of all *tikkun*. From that moment, there will no longer be a need for the letter *Tet* to bring additional souls to the world.

On *Tisha B'Av*, the Holy Temple was taken from us, yet this is the day on which Messiah is born. That is why *Tisha B'Av* is not just a day of mourning, as is commonly perceived. The paradoxical combination of the Destruction and the redemption on the same day is connected to that quality of *Yesod* which is revealed on the ninth day of every month. Anyone who learns the *Ten Luminous Emanations* knows that each time we are faced with paradox, we are discussing an aspect of true reality. In fact, if something is not paradoxical, it is an illusion!

One aspect of *Tisha B'Av*'s paradox is that despite the fact that it is a holiday and the birthday of Messiah, we implement the five restrictions—the very same ones we use on *Yom Kippur*. These restrictions—no eating, drinking, wearing leather shoes, engaging in sexual relations, or bathing—enable us to achieve a much higher connection to the Light so that we can control our destinies and the destiny of the entire universe: control that makes it possible to eradicate every aspect of chaos from the world. *Tisha B'Av*, in contrast, is a seemingly regular day on which we are unable to approach high spiritual levels. Then why must we observe the five prohibitions, and what actually takes place on *Tisha B'Av*?

The Zohar teaches us that the Holy Temple was never destroyed. So what are the Jews mourning about? Anyone who has not learned the *Ten Luminous Emanations* will certainly ask why we can't see the Holy Temple; anyone who has learned knows that the senses expose only the neglected part of the reality that surrounds us. The fact that we do not see the *Beit Hamikdash* (The Holy Temple) does not mean that it does not exist. We do not see radio waves, but that does not mean that they do not exist. Does *Tisha B'Av* exist for the sole purpose of reminding us of the Israelites suffering in Jerusalem during the Destruction? The people of Israel have suffered many hardships; if we were to be reminded of them all, the entire year would be full of mourning and solemnity.

The destruction of the physical Holy Temple could not have happened without a causal connection to *Tisha B'Av*. This special energetic situation can manifest either in the Destruction of the Temple or in the birth of Messiah—a view completely different from the traditional conception of *Tisha B'Av*. No single person can achieve this understanding of his own accord, for it is beyond the bounds of the senses and the physical mind. We require help on a global level from an external source—and this source is the Creator. Kabbalistic wisdom has been handed down to us from the Creator by means of Moses, documented in the cosmic codes known as the Torah, *The Zohar*, and *The Book of Formation*. They provide us with wisdom and internal understanding of the universe: which days are positive, which days are negative, which days energy is broadcast throughout the universe, and during which days we can receive cosmic support.

Was there a reason for choosing this day in the month of *Av* for the cosmic event in which chaos has control? How can we understand this timing? As we know, two months in the year—*Tammuz* and *Av*—offer us a double dose of energy compared to the rest of the months. Five planets bestow their might on two zodiac signs, which nourish ten months of the year. In contrast, the moon concentrates all of its power on *Tammuz*, and the Sun concentrates all of its energy on *Av*. Consequently, these two months can manifest things that no other month is capable of manifesting. It is no coincidence that the energy of *Tammuz* is channeled to the universe through the sign of Cancer, as the sign bears a name that strikes fear into the hearts of all people. The negative power of the illness comes from the power that the moon reveals through the sign. Depending on each person's consciousness, the month of *Tammuz* can result in disease or in perfect health. The destiny that manifests the illness is determined by the quality of the seed planted in *Tammuz*.

Cancer is a water sign. *Av*, conversely, is fire sign. They are two interdependent entities. Water can be very positive, but when its energy manifests with an excess of judgment, it can be lethal. Fire can be positive and beneficial, but when revealed in excess in an unrestrained manner—in judgment—there is nothing more destructive. In *Tammuz*, the power of water is revealed with judgment, and in *Av* the power of fire is revealed with judgment. Kabbalah teaches us ways to govern those negative forces to connect in a balanced way to the positive energy revealed in these months and to harness this energy for our benefit. Without this knowledge, we are doomed to suffer and possibly be harmed at these times.

There is no room for religiosity in the world—in any spiritual framework. The Israelite sustains the entire world with the Light of the Creator; as long as the Israelite remains in the dark, as long as the Israelite does not uphold "love thy neighbor as thyself," there will always be conflict, violence, and ecological problems throughout the world. But if on *Tisha B'Av* we take it upon ourselves to restrict the desire to receive for the self alone, and through the five prohibitions we convert our longing for instant gratification into a desire to share with all of the earth's inhabitants, a true change in the course of history can begin to take place on this day. That is how we can bring the Final Redemption to fruition. That is how Messiah is born.

We do not mourn the Temple on *Tisha B'Av*, for the Temple was never destroyed. Its physical appearance has simply been concealed from our view. What was destroyed and what we should mourn is the loss of the spiritual Temple—the metaphysical vessel found in the heart of every Isrealite in the world. But the way to mourn the destruction of the metaphysical vessel is not to fall into a deep depression, but instead to restrict, via the five prohibitions, the desire to receive that brought about the Destruction. We must then connect with happiness and love to the Tree of Life and responsibly channel the Light that is revealed on this day to all Creation.

That is why Rav Shimon Bar Yochai, in *Portion Beha'alot'cha* of *The Zohar*, said that those who live in the Age of Aquarius have a great opportunity but are also at great risk—for it is this generation that will welcome the Messiah. Woe is the person who lives at that time, or praiseworthy is that person—the answer is up to us. Those who are able to connect with the Light in a balanced manner will merit the coming of Messiah and experience all the blessings he deserves. Those who do not understand the message that the Torah provides will find that their situation worsens day by day.

On the eve of *Tisha B'Av*, we read from *The Zohar*'s section called *Megillat Eicha*—the strongest connection to the positive energy revealed on the holiday. Those who do not understand Aramaic can connect to the energy concentrated in the text simply by scanning the letters. Only the power of the Aramaic alphabet is capable of connecting us to the spiritual energy broadcast throughout the universe. Only the Aramaic letters are capable of channeling the Light our way. By virtue of this visual scanning, our minds are directed and are able to manifest the positive potential concentrated in the Light.

The reading of *Megillat Eicha* allows us to learn that the true reason for the Destruction was hatred for no reason amongst the Jews. Every person is capable of hating someone who hurts him; this is normal. But only hatred for no reason can cause the Holy Temple to disappear from the eyes of most people in the world. In the process of our connection to the tremendous power of *Tisha B'Av*, we must take it upon ourselves to cleanse and drive out from our midst all fragmentation and any trace of hatred, for hatred toward others only connects the hater to chaos and judgment. That is why we must try not to hate a single person. Soon, in the time of Messiah, people will love their neighbors as freely as they hate today, for no reason at all. The situation of love for no reason was prevalent amongst the Israelites on *Purim*, and will prevail once again in Messiah's time. I am not trying to persuade you to feel warmth and concern toward people that you do not know, but in our immediate surroundings, we should make the effort to erase any trace of hatred from within us. As long as people are in touch with hatred, he will be unable to connect to the energy of life that is revealed on *Tisha B'Av*.

On the eve of *Tisha B'Av*, we sit by candlelight and not by electrical light. Tradition says this is a symbol of mourning. However, we light candles on festive occasions, before Shabbat and holidays. In expensive restaurants, patrons dim the lights and eat by candlelight. On *Tisha B'Av*, we connect to the festive side of the candle, its white flame—not to its negative side, the sooty wick. This is the assurance we receive from Kabbalah.

We sit on the floor and meditate to draw energy that is not available at any other time of the year—to fill the world with health, order, harmony and life. Not only do we sit on the floor, but we also fast, we do not wear leather shoes, we do not engage in sexual relations, and we do not bathe or apply creams and lotions, just as on *Yom Kippur*. Leather shoes insulate us from the energy of the ground. Because we are so concerned with connecting with the ground, we choose not to wear leather shoes. The drawing power of the ground is expressed physically by the kabbalistic spiritual quality known as *Malchut*, signified by the desire to receive. When we sit on the floor on *Tisha B'Av*, we connect to the power of *Malchut* and, by means of the earth, we can go back and connect to the Light of the Creator, which we were previously able to draw only by means of the Holy Temple. We must elevate ourselves to an alternative consciousness from which Rav Shimon notified us that the Holy Temple was never truly destroyed. The Temple exists only for those who know how to connect to it.

This consciousness is the key to redemption. It is also the explanation for the argument over who is worthy of reading *Megillat Eicha*. The true meaning of the question is this: Who is capable, by means of the order of the *Aleph-Bet* of the verses in *Megillat Eicha*, to bring about the Final Redemption? The answer is: Only those who see that all expressions of chaos are only illusory. They are literally able to see the Holy Temple standing on Mount Moriah. We must concentrate on the connection inherent in *Tisha B'Av* to bring Messiah consciousness to the world and drive out any aspect of chaos. And the only way to remove chaos is by knowing that chaos really does not exist.

Tu B'Av
(15TH OF LEO)

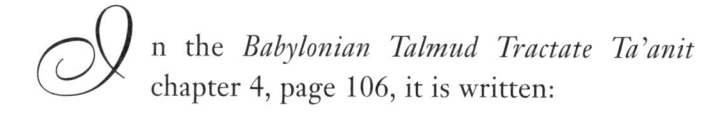

In the *Babylonian Talmud Tractate Ta'anit* chapter 4, page 106, it is written:

> Rabbi Shimon Ben Gamliel said, 'There are no better days in Israel than *Tu B'Av* and *Yom Kippur*. On *Tu B'Av* the daughters of Jerusalem go out dressed in borrowed white clothes, so that those who lack garments are clothed, and they celebrate in the vineyards. And what do they say? 'Boy, raise your eyes and see what a selection you have! Let your eyes not gaze upon us ornaments, but let your eyes seek a family.'

This idea of borrowing clothes from one another contributes to the respect for the poor and strengthens the feeling of unity and love amid the people. This is an unusual custom, and it is one that is not mentioned in reference to any other holiday. The *Talmud* goes on to describe additional aspects of young men coming to choose a soul mate. This is the first description of *Tu B'Av* that we encounter, except for the description that appears in the *Kitvei H'Ari*.

On this day, we are promised that we will find soul mates and merit happy marital lives. But why on this of all days? The Jerusalem *Talmud* and The Ari explain the connection between *Tu B'Av* and *Yom Kippur*. They say that a man who marries a woman for the sake of heaven—whose marriage is not for the desire to receive for the self alone but rather to contribute to the *tikkun* of the entire universe—merits the same erasure of sins that takes place on *Yom Kippur*. While some marry for beauty or wealth, there are also those who seek a soul mate for the sake of advancing the personal and global *tikkun* process. A relationship for the sake of heaven supports *Zeir Anpin* consciousness, the desire to share abundance with the world, and therefore strengthens the entire universe.

There is exactly one half year between *Tu B'Av* and *Tu Bishvat*. These two festivals oppose one another like the north and south poles of the earth. *Tu Bishvat* is considered a "little holiday" because there are no special *mitzvot* connected with it, no special Torah reading, and no fasts or prohibitions. But anyone who thinks that it is truly a little holiday is sorely mistaken. The source of the events that are connected to this holiday is rooted in a place beyond the frame of the senses and the material world, just like *Purim*. The *mitzvah* most commonly associated with this holiday is that of inebriation to the point of incoherence, a practice that is considered sinful on any other day. There is a close connection between *Tu Bishvat* (the sign of Aquarius, an air sign) and *Tu B'Av* (the sign of Leo, a fire sign). These two signs, air and fire, support and complement one another, and each carries great significance. They both fall on the 15th of the month, when the moon is full and shining on us with the totality of the sun's Light without any interference. The fact that the moon appears full from the earth's perspective attests to the unification of *Zeir Anpin* and *Malchut* on the 15th day of the month. Therefore, the 15th of every month is ideal for new beginnings.

Tu B'Av is the best of all, because it is the day on which the full force of the sun, of *Zeir Anpin*, is revealed. This is the source of power for the sign of Leo and the reason that the lion is king of the jungle. The lion is the channel for the revelation of *Zeir Anpin* energy in the world. The energies of thought consciousness that lead the world come down in abundance through a system of channels. In the beginning, they manifest on a planetary level. Then they are expressed through the signs, and finally they actualize on the earth's surface. The lion, like every person born under the influence of the sign of Leo, is a channel connecting us directly to the system that provides the world with the energy of *Zeir Anpin*, both positively by supporting life and negatively by creating death and destruction.

On *Tu B'Av*, a union begins between the sun and the moon. The power of the sun is revealed in the month of *Av*, causing the greatest revelation of Light upon us. Therefore, on *Tu B'Av*, this union gives us greater power than any other time of the year. A disharmonious connection with the sun's power can bring a holocaust upon the world, as we saw each time the Holy Temple was burned. The Destruction of the Temple was only an external expression of the destructive and chaotic pattern that the world had fallen into. There is no room for distinction between the good of the Israelite and the good of the world. When the Israelite suffers, the entire universe suffers. The world has yet to witness a situation that has been bad for the Israelite good for the rest of the world. If the Israelite draws judgment to the world, all of earth's inhabitants are subject to this judgment. If the Israelite draws negative energy into the world, the whole world is afflicted. But if the Israelite reveals Light in a balanced way, all of humanity walks upright while the animals crawl on the ground. When a person feels good, he behaves in a positive way. That is why the responsibility of humanity's behavior rests in the hands of the Israelite and his/her actions.

There is a strong connection and similarity between *Tu B'Av* and *Tu Bishvat*, the New Year of the Trees. The internal energy of the tree is *Zeir Anpin*, the desire to share with others. Therefore, the tree is not subject to the desire to receive for the self alone, as is characteristic of the earth's gravitational pull, and that is why it grows upward. In addition, by means of photosynthesis, trees tirelessly purify and recycle the air that we breathe. Researchers have found that without the "green lung" of Central Park, life could not exist in New York. This is the importance and significance of trees, and that is why the New Year of the Trees happens under the control of an air sign. We plant trees on *Tu Bishvat* because at that time there is cosmic support for the energy of sharing, or *Zeir Anpin*. On *Tu B'Av*, *Malchut* is given the opportunity to connect to the consciousness of *Zeir Anpin*, represented in the universe by the sun and expressed on earth by the vegetable kingdom.

Av is the most negative of the three negative months of the year. In these months, we are cautioned not to begin anything new even on Tuesdays, which are usually considered positive days. The amount of Light revealed could overwhelm us like a flood. And just as there can be a flood of water, there can also be a flood of fire. That is why we take such precautionary measures during *Av*. According to *The Zohar*, *Av* is a dangerous period because of the high level of energy transmitted throughout the universe. The energy itself is not negative, but its tremendous strength is more than our vessels can handle without being damaged. This law applies to the entire month except for one day: *Tu B'Av*. In general, we refrain from starting new things in the second half of every Lunar month. But on *Tu B'Av*, there is a complete unification between *Zeir Anpin* and *Malchut*, offering balanced cosmic support for every relationship and every new beginning. That is why this day is good to marry and begin business ventures. The *Talmud* tells us that because this day offers us a balanced dose of the sun's energy and the energy of Leo, it makes *Tu B'Av* similar in nature to *Purim*, the only holiday that we will celebrate forever.

The Ari teaches us that seven positive events took place on *Tu B'Av*, corresponding to the Seven *Sfirot*. We have also learned that when something manifests through the Seven *Sfirot* from *Chesed* to *Malchut* (see Diagram 3), it receives completeness in our world. The seven positive events happened on this day for the sake of fulfilling and activating the total connection between the Light and the vessel.

One of these seven events was the forgiveness of the Tribe of Benjamin's sin and the bestowal of permission to intermarry with that tribe. This event expresses a manifestation of unity that is the focal consciousness of the day. Practically speaking, it is the only day that is actually perfect for beginning new ventures or creating unity of any kind. According to *The Zohar*, the other positive day in which there is unity between *Zeir Anpin* and *Malchut* is the first of *Cheshvan*, during which a huge amount of life energy is injected into the world. But it is still not comparable to *Tu B'Av*. *Cheshvan* is controlled by the sign of Scorpio, making its name *Mar-Cheshvan*, or bitter *Cheshvan*. Why is this the case? Because the Great Flood began in the month of *Cheshvan*. And why did the Flood begin precisely in this month? Because in *Cheshvan* the heavenly powers create a spiritual environment in which a flood can take place. There are no holidays in *Cheshvan*. Why go to the extent to call the month of *Cheshvan* bitter, or *Mar*? Was the slaughter of thousands and the Destruction of the Temple not bitter enough? The month of *Av* is not called bitter, but rather the opposite; it is called *Menachem-Av*, the month of consolation.

The solution to these complexities lies in the congruence between the vessel and the Light. In *Cheshvan*, tremendous Light is revealed, but the vessel is not appropriate, and that is the reason for the Great Deluge. *Tu B'Av* enables a perfect fit between the Light and the vessel, facilitating a great revelation of Light—and that is why this month holds the key to Redemption, to consolation, and the bringing of Messiah. On *Pesach* (Passover) there is a paradox. *Nissan* can be a negative month if we do not connect to the energy that is transmitted on the evening of the *Seder* and do not reveal it in the world with the right consciousness, in the way that Kabbalah teaches us. If we are not in harmony with the universe, then we are subject to the negative aspect of any month. The Torah tells us (*Deuteronomy* 30:19), "And I give you life and death—choose life."

On the 15th of Nissan, we must perform *mitzvot* in order to connect to the Light, even if we love organic whole—wheat bread. But on *Tu B'Av*, there is no need to observe any restrictions in order to manifest the potential concealed in the Light. All the goodness that is potentially in *Nissan* is revealed in *Av*. In order to connect to the Light in *Nissan*, we must engage in specific actions out of choice or intention. In *Av*, the connection takes place regardless. On this day, we celebrate with just understanding *Tu B'Av*'s significance. That's it; nothing else is required. On this holiday, we can connect to the Light without any effort. Therefore, *Tu B'Av* is great for finding matches and great happiness.

On *Tu B'Av*, the daughters of Jerusalem used to go out wearing white and celebrate in the vineyards with a circular dance. The consciousness that the young women had on *Tu B'Av* was that of a circle: the consciousness of eternity, sanctity, and a balanced flow of energy—which is exactly the consciousness of the perfect union between *Zeir Anpin* and *Malchut*. Circular consciousness is connected above all else to *Or Makif*, or surrounding light—the consciousness that unifies and embraces the entire universe, which is expressed in a quantum dimension. By means of this consciousness, we can achieve total unity with all creations in the universe. This enables us to remove chaos from the world and merit true and lasting fulfillment. Therefore, this is the ideal consciousness for finding your soul mate. With the help of this consciousness, we are able to find our soul mates for marriage, as well as business partners and friends. The connection to the energy that is transmitted throughout the universe on *Tu B'Av* facilitates the sustenance, strengthening, balance, and healing of all relationships.

But if the energy of *Tu B'Av* is so universal, why does the *Talmud* speak only of the daughters of Jerusalem? Why don't all the women of the world wear their finest clothes, regardless of color? After all, each woman has a different color that suits her best. The Ari answers these questions and others, explaining that the *Talmud*, like the Torah, gives us only hints and allusions. The secret of the connection between *Tu B'Av* and *Yom Kippur* is the idea that at the end of prayers on *Yom Kippur*, the congregants cry out "*Hashem Hu Ha'Elokim*" (Hashem is Elokim). This statement refers to the unification between *Zeir Anpin* (the Tetragrammaton) and *Malchut* (Elokim). And that is what happens throughout the universe on *Tu B'Av* as well.

The Ari explains that *Tu B'Av* feeds *Binah*, just as *Yom Kippur* does. On *Yom Kippur*, *Zeir Anpin* and *Malchut* meet in *Binah*, in the universal storehouse of spiritual energy. It is not every day that we can reach *Binah*. But on *Tu B'Av* and *Yom Kippur*, it is possible. On these days the moon does not require the sun in order to shine, but instead receives its Light directly from *Binah* without the thinning or filtration of *Zeir Anpin*, thereby acting just like the sun. And when we speak about the moon, we are also referring to ourselves and the rest of the earth's inhabitants in the world of physical illusion, the world of chaos, and Murphy's laws. On these two days, the Light of *Binah* pierces the veils and sustains anyone who wants to connect to it, without diminution, in the same immensity that sustains the sun. But in order to accomplish this, we must first be aware of it. Those who think that on *Tu B'Av* the Light of the moon is nothing but a reflection of the sun's rays, just like any other night of the year, are not able to receive the energy of this powerful day and consequently are unable to achieve mind over matter. After this explanation, the connection between *Tu B'Av* and *Yom Kippur* is clear. This connection also gives *Tu B'Av* another meaning: Just as on *Yom Kippur* we are able to be forgiven and absolved of all sins, so too are we given this chance on *Tu B'Av*.

The Ari goes on to explain why the daughters of Jerusalem went out into the vineyards. Vineyards connect us to the energy of wine. Wine, as we know, is the tool to connect to the spiritual energy that is transmitted in the universe. That is the connection we make at every *Kiddush*. A vineyard is the perfect expression of the World of Truth. In other words, the young women did not actually have to go to the vineyards, and they did not have to travel from Jerusalem to Zichron Yaacov; in consciousness, they had to manifest the special energy of the day—the energy of a total and harmonious connection between *Zeir Anpin* and *Malchut*. This takes place when a couple marries and is also the condition of the cosmos on *Yom Kippur*. Therefore, on their wedding day, a bride and groom can achieve their *tikkun* and be purified of all of their previous sins. A wedding day is like a personal *Yom Kippur* for the bride and groom, and that is why they customarily fast on the day before the wedding.

Purim is of an even higher level than *Yom Kippur*. On *Purim* we can reach *Chochmah*, the storehouse that sustains *Binah*. But in order to do that, we must hear the reading of *Megillat Esther* and transform our consciousness to that of the Israelites of Shushan 3,000 years ago. On *Purim*, they formed a perfect connection with the Light, which enabled all people who lived at that time to complete their *tikkun*. *Tu B'Av* is not as powerful but is capable of establishing a spiritual infrastructure that will ultimately enable us to complete our *tikkun*, despite the fact that we are not required to do any specific actions or be party to readings of *Megillot* or the Torah. In order for us to prevent the accumulation of

Bread of Shame, there is but one requirement: We must first establish within ourselves a spiritual vessel to handle the tremendous Light so that it works in our favor. And this vessel has but one source: the consciousness of unity. This is the reason the Tribe of Benjamin was able to reunite with the rest of Israel on *Tu B'Av*. Through the lack of unity between the tribes, there was no possibility of connecting to the energy that is revealed in the universe on *Tu B'Av*. Separation leads to chaos. Certainty and continuity lead to unity. These elements are equally interdependent in that the consciousness of unity and the fulfillment of "love your thy neighbor as thyself" are key to removing chaos from our lives and manifesting continuity and certainty. In order to awaken within us the power of unity and to prepare the vessel for the Light of *Tu B'Av*, we hold a special event that must include a meal. We should also remember this spiritual vessel is also the precursor for bringing Messiah to the world and manifesting the Redemption with mercy.

Rav Shimon said that there is but one way of lighting the Torah's path, bringing Messiah to the world and manifesting the Redemption with mercy. That way is *The Zohar*. Life without *The Zohar* is like driving at night without headlights. Without the guidance of *The Zohar*, we are unable to see the signs leading our way and cannot know where to turn, so we proceed down the road of life very slowly. Without *The Zohar*, we cannot understand the *Talmud* and cannot know that the vineyard is not just a place where grapes are grown. Only *The Zohar* tells us that vineyard is code for the consciousness of *Zeir Anpin*. We must bring *The Zohar* into our lives so as to light the signs alongside the road and to banish the darkness and chaos from our lives.

Diagram #1

The Upper Realm

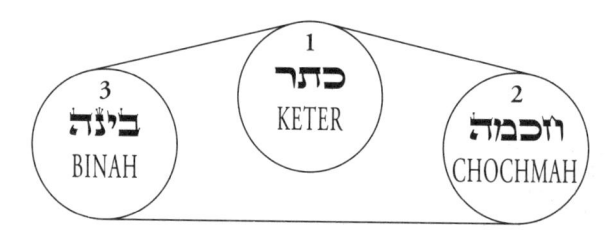

- 1 כתר KETER
- 2 חכמה CHOCHMAH
- 3 בינה BINAH

The Seven Sfirot

LEFT COLUMN   **CENTRAL COLUMN**   **RIGHT COLUMN**

- 4 חסד CHESED
- 5 גבורה GVURAH
- 6 תפארת TIFERET
- 7 נצח NETZACH
- 8 הוד HOD
- 9 יסוד YESOD
- 10 מלכות MALCHUT

Diagram #2

The Upper Realm

- 10 כתר KETER
- 8 בִּינָה BINAH
- 9 וְחָכְמָה CHOCHMAH

The Seven Sfirot

LEFT COLUMN — CENTRAL COLUMN — RIGHT COLUMN

- 6 גְּבוּרָה GVURAH
- 5 תִּפְאֶרֶת TIFERET
- 7 וְחֶסֶד CHESED
- 3 הוֹד HOD
- 2 יְסוֹד YESOD
- 4 נֵצַח NETZACH
- 1 מַלְכוּת MALCHUT

Diagram #3

The Upper Realm

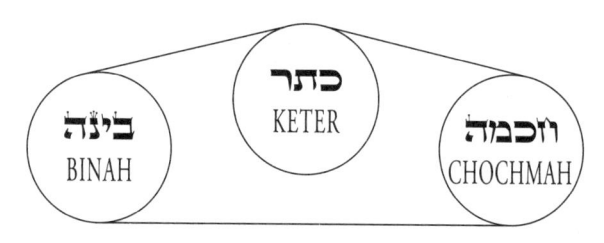

- בינה BINAH
- כתר KETER
- וזכמה CHOCHMAH

The Seven Sfirot

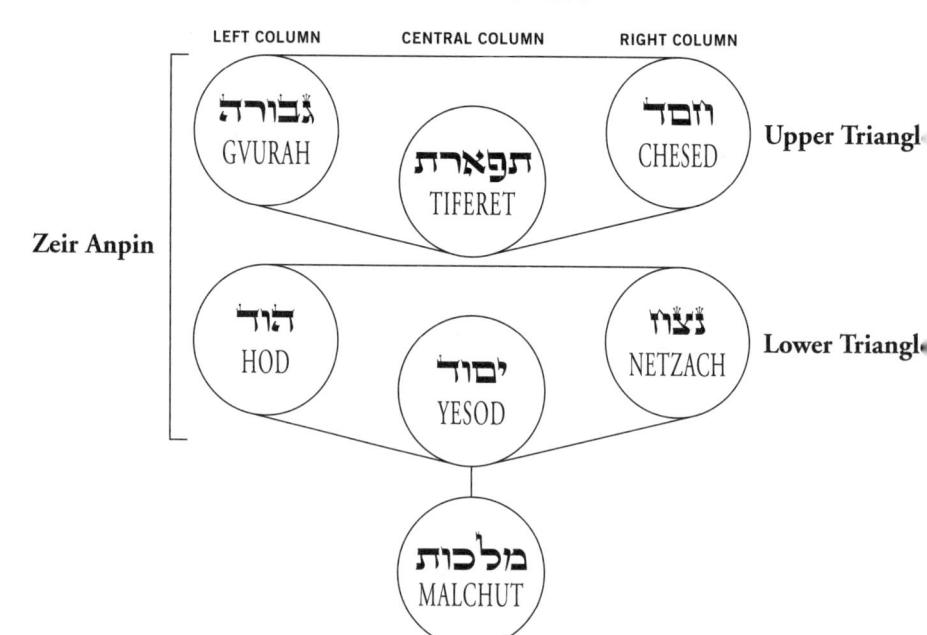

LEFT COLUMN — CENTRAL COLUMN — RIGHT COLUMN

Zeir Anpin

- גבורה GVURAH
- תפארת TIFERET
- וזסד CHESED

Upper Triangle

- הוד HOD
- יסוד YESOD
- נצוז NETZACH

Lower Triangle

- מלכות MALCHUT

Diagram #4

The Upper Realm

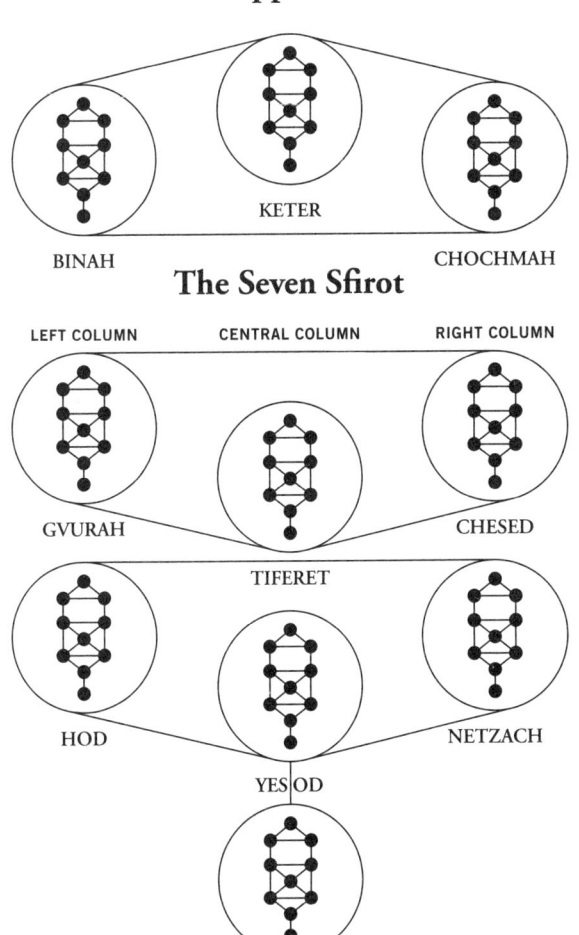

BINAH KETER CHOCHMAH

The Seven Sfirot

LEFT COLUMN CENTRAL COLUMN RIGHT COLUMN

GVURAH CHESED

TIFERET

HOD NETZACH

YESOD

Diagram #5

Seder Plate

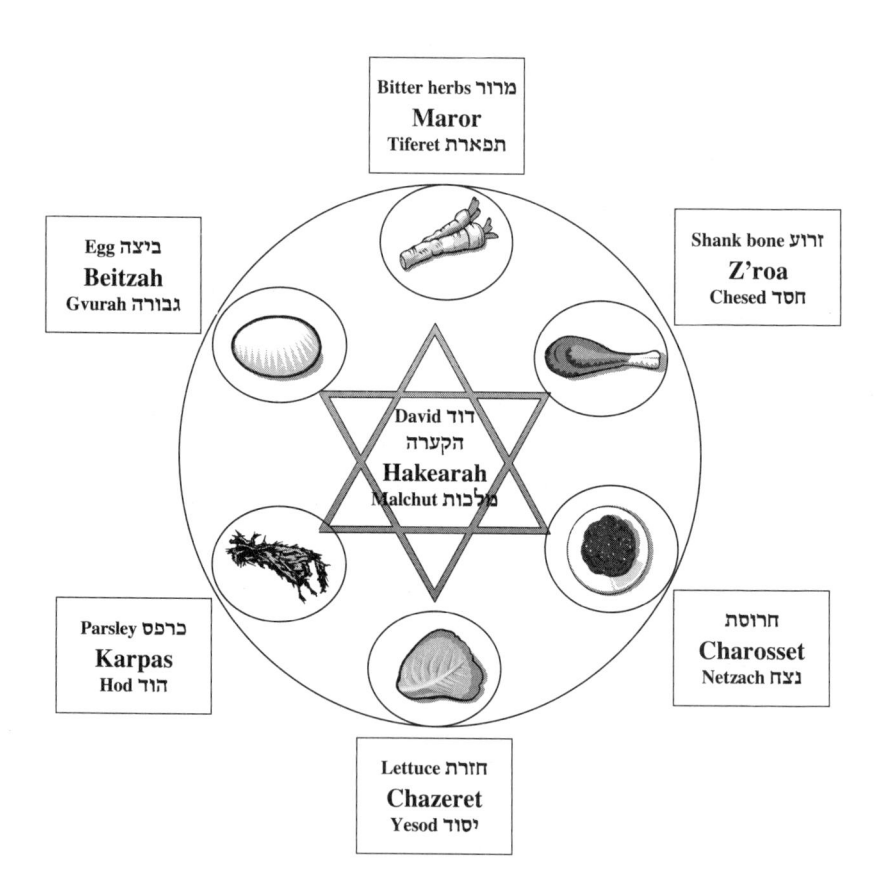

Bitter herbs מרור
Maror
Tiferet תפארת

Egg ביצה
Beitzah
Gvurah גבורה

Shank bone זרוע
Z'roa
Chesed חסד

David דוד
הקערה
Hakearah
Malchut מלכות

חרוסת
Charosset
Netzach נצח

Parsley כרפס
Karpas
Hod הוד

Lettuce חזרת
Chazeret
Yesod יסוד

Diagram #6

Tikkun Hanefesh

Left Brain מוח שמאל **Binah** בינה יְהֹוָה 3	**Skull** גלגתא **Keter** כתר יָהָוָהָ 1	**Right Brain** מוח ימין **Chochmah** חכמה יַהַוַהַ 2
Left Eye עין שמאל 5 יהוה יהוה יהוה יהוה יהוה	**Nose** חוטם יְ יְ יִ יִ יֱ יֱ יִ יִ	**Right Eye** עין ימין 4 יהוה יהוה יהוה יהוה יהוה
Left Ear אזן שמאל 7 יוד הי ואו הה	9 8	**Right Ear** אזן ימין 6 יוד הי ואו הה
Mouth פה 10 יוד הי ואו הי (אהיה) אחה"ע גיכ"ק דטלנ"ת זסשר"ץ בומ"ף		
Left Arm זרוע שמאל **Gvurah** גבורה יְהֹוִה 12	**Body** גוף **Tiferet** תפארת יֱהֱוֱהֱ 13	**Right Arm** זרוע ימין **Chased** חסד יְהֹוָה 11
Left Leg ירך שמאל **Hod** הוד יְהֹוִה 15	**Reproductive Organs** **Yesod** יסוד יוּ הוּ וּוּ הוּ 16	**Right Leg** ירך ימין **Netzach** נצח יְהֹוָה 14
	Feet **Malchut** עטרה מלכות יהוה 17	

273

More from Rav P. S. Berg

Wheels of a Soul
By Rav Berg

In *Wheels of a Soul*, Kabbalist Rav Berg reveals the keys to answering these and many more questions that lie at the heart of our existence as human beings. Specifically, Rav Berg explains why we must acknowledge and explore the lives we have already lived in order to understand the life we are living today...

Make no mistake: *you have been here before*. Reincarnation is a fact—and just as science is now beginning to recognize that time and space may be nothing but illusions, Rav Berg shows why death itself is the greatest illusion of all.

In this book you learn much more than the answers to these questions. You will understand your true purpose in the world and discover tools to identify your life's soul mate. Read *Wheels of a Soul* and let one of the greatest kabbalistic masters of our time change your life forever.

The Power of You
By Rav Berg

For the past 5,000 years, neither science nor psychology has been able to solve the fundamental problem of chaos in people's lives.

Now, one man is providing the answer. He is Kabbalist Rav Berg.

Beneath the pain and chaos that disrupts our lives, Kabbalist Rav Berg brings to light a hidden realm of order, purpose, and unity. Revealed is a universe in which mind becomes master over matter—a world in which God, human thought, and the entire cosmos are mysteriously interconnected.

Join this generation's premier kabbalist on a mind-bending journey along the cutting edge of reality. Peer into the vast reservoir of spiritual wisdom that is Kabbalah, where the secrets of creation, life, and death have remained hidden for thousands of years.

The Essential Zohar
By Rav Berg

The Zohar has traditionally been known as the world's most esoteric and profound spiritual document, but Kabbalist Rav Berg, this generation's greatest living Kabbalist, has dedicated his life to making this wisdom universally available. The vast wisdom and Light of *The Zohar* came into being as a gift to all humanity, and *The Essential Zohar* at last explains this gift to the world.

The Kabbalah Method
By Rav Berg

The Kabbalah Method reveals the dual aspect of Kabbalah as spirituality and a science. Previously arcane aspects of Kabbalah such as The Four Phases of Creation, The Ten Sefirot, and The Circle and The Line, become crystal clear as they come to life in these pages. As you read about them, you will see the spiritual system of Kabbalah unfold and will know that you are in the presence of one of the world's great spiritual teachings. But, this book does far more than recount philosophical or intellectual ideas. Rather, it reveals the powerful, practical tools that have helped untold numbers of people achieve greater fulfillment and understanding in every area of their lives. Simply put, *The Kabbalah Method* is 4,000 years of wisdom in a single enlightening volume. This is a must-read for everyone who hungers to know more about the timeless foundations of the universe—and who yearns for a fulfilled and joyous life full of meaning.

THE ZOHAR

"Bringing *The Zohar* from near oblivion to wide accessibility has taken many decades. It is an achievement of which we are truly proud and grateful."

—Michael Berg

Composed more than 2,000 years ago, *The Zohar* is a set of 23 books, a commentary on biblical and spiritual matters in the form of conversations among spiritual masters. But to describe *The Zohar* only in physical terms is greatly misleading. In truth, *The Zohar* is nothing less than a powerful tool for achieving the most important purposes of our lives. It was given to all humankind by the Creator to bring us protection, to connect us with the Creator's Light, and ultimately to fulfill our birthright of true spiritual transformation.

More than eighty years ago, when The Kabbalah Centre was founded, *The Zohar* had virtually disappeared from the world. Few people in the general population had ever heard of it. Whoever sought to read it—in any country, in any language, at any price—faced a long and futile search.

Today all this has changed. Through the work of The Kabbalah Centre and the editorial efforts of Michael Berg, *The Zohar* is now being brought to the world, not only in the original Aramaic language but also in English.

The new English *Zohar* provides everything for connecting to this sacred text on all levels: the original Aramaic text for scanning; an English translation; and clear, concise commentary for study and learning.

More Books that can bring the Wisdom of Kabbalah into your Life

God Wears Lipstick
By Karen Berg

God Wears Lipstick is written exclusively for women (or for men who better want to understand women) by one of the driving forces behind the Kabbalah movement.

For thousands of years, women were banned from studying Kabbalah, the ancient source of wisdom that explains who we are and what our purpose is in this universe.

Karen Berg changed that. She opened the doors of The Kabbalah Centre to anyone who wanted to understand the wisdom of Kabbalah and brought Light to these people.

In *God Wears Lipstick*, Karen Berg shares that wisdom with us, especially as it affects you and your relationships. She reveals a woman's special place in the universe and why women have a spiritual advantage over men. She explains how to find your soulmate and your purpose in life. She empowers you to become a better human being as you connect to the Light, and she then gives you the tools for living and loving.

The Power of Kabbalah
By Yehuda Berg

Imagine your life filled with unending joy, purpose, and contentment. Imagine your days infused with pure insight and energy. This is *The Power of Kabbalah*. It is the path from the momentary pleasure that most of us settle for, to the lasting fulfillment that is yours to claim. Your deepest desires are waiting to be realized. But they are not limited to the temporary rush from closing a business deal, the short-term high from drugs, or a passionate sexual relationship that lasts only a few short months.

Wouldn't you like to experience a lasting sense of wholeness and peace that is unshakable, no matter what may be happening around you? Complete fulfillment is the promise of Kabbalah. Within these pages, you will learn how to look at and navigate through life in a whole new way. You will understand your purpose and how to receive the abundant gifts waiting for you. By making a critical transformation from a reactive to a proactive being, you will increase your creative energy, get control of your life, and enjoy new spiritual levels of existence. Kabbalah's ancient teaching is rooted in the perfect union of the physical and spiritual laws already at work in your life. Get ready to experience this exciting realm of awareness, meaning, and joy.

The wonder and wisdom of Kabbalah has influenced the world's leading spiritual, philosophical, religious, and scientific minds. Until today, however, it was hidden away in ancient texts, available only to scholars who knew where to look. Now after many centuries, *The Power of Kabbalah* resides right here in this one remarkable book. Here, at long last is the complete and simple path—actions you can take right now to create the life you desire and deserve.

The 72 Names of God: Technology for the Soul™
By Yehuda Berg

The story of Moses and the Red Sea is well known to almost everyone; it's even been an Academy Award–winning film. What is not known, according to the internationally prominent author Yehuda Berg, is that a state-of-the-art technology is encoded and concealed within that biblical story. This technology is called the 72 Names of God, and it is the key—your key—to ridding yourself of depression, stress, creative stagnation, anger, illness, and other physical and emotional problems. In fact, the 72 Names of God is the oldest, most powerful tool known to mankind—far more powerful than any 21st century high-tech know-how when it comes to eliminating the garbage in your life so that you can wake up and enjoy life each day. Indeed, the 72 Names of God is the ultimate pill for anything and everything that ails you because it strikes at the DNA level of your soul.

The power of the 72 Names of God operates strictly on a soul level, not a physical one. It's about spirituality, not religiosity. Rather than being limited by the differences that divide people, the wisdom of the Names transcends humanity's age-old quarrels and belief systems to deal with the one common bond that unifies all people and nations: the human soul.

It's all here. Everything you wanted to know about the Red String but were afraid to ask!

Becoming Like God
By Michael Berg

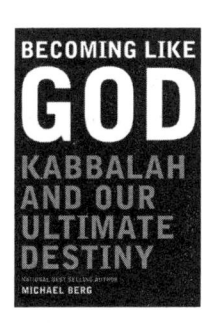

At the age of 16, kabbalistic scholar Michael Berg began the herculean task of translating *The Zohar*, Kabbalah's chief text, from its original Aramaic into its first complete English translation. *The Zohar*, which consists of 23 volumes, is considered a compendium of virtually all information pertaining to the universe, and its wisdom is only beginning to be verified today.

During the ten years he worked on *The Zohar*, Michael Berg discovered the long-lost secret for which humanity has searched for more than 5,000 years: how to achieve our ultimate destiny. *Becoming Like God* reveals the transformative method by which people can actually break free of what is called "ego nature" to achieve total joy and lasting life.

Berg puts forth the revolutionary idea that for the first time in history, an opportunity is being made available to humankind: an opportunity to Become Like God.

The Secret
By Michael Berg

Like a jewel that has been painstakingly cut and polished, *The Secret* reveals life's essence in its most concise and powerful form. Michael Berg begins by showing you how our everyday understanding of our purpose in the world is literally backwards. Whenever there is pain in our lives—indeed, whenever there is anything less than complete joy and fulfillment—this basic misunderstanding is the reason.

The Kabbalah Centre

The International Leader in the Education of Kabbalah

Since its founding, The Kabbalah Centre has had a single mission: to improve and transform people's lives by bringing the power and wisdom of Kabbalah to all who wish to partake of it.

Through the lifelong efforts of Kabbalists Rav and Karen Berg, and the great spiritual lineage of which they are a part, an astonishing 3.5 million people around the world have already been touched by the powerful teachings of Kabbalah. And each year, the numbers are growing!

• • • •

If you were inspired by this book in any way and would like to know how you can continue to enrich your life through the wisdom of Kabbalah, here is what you can do next:

Call 1-800-KABBALAH where trained instructors are available 18 hours a day. These dedicated people are willing to answer any and all questions about Kabbalah and help guide you along in your effort to learn more.

May the days of power and the wisdom of this book bring all of us closer to reuniting as one soul with the Light force of the Creator in the Endless World—me with my soul mate and you with yours—in a place of total and eternal fulfillment.

—Janice Hope

The Light is calling to the consciousness of all humanity to awaken from slumber and to take action to stop the chaos, the pain, and the suffering of humanity. May each of us be guided to seek and learn the truth and to put into practice the teaching of "love thy neighbor as thyself."

May the Light that shines in our souls manifest in our lives and the lives of our families and friends. With gratitude to Harav and Karen.

—Richard and Karen Macedonio